CULT HEROES

First published in Great Britain in 1989
by André Deutsch Limited

Library of Congress Cataloging-in-Publication Data

Sudjic, Deyan.
   Cult heroes: how to be famous for more than fifteen minutes/
  Deyan Sudjic.
     p. cm.
   1. Popular culture—Marketing. 2. Celebrities. I. Title.
  CB 430. S83 1990
  659. 1'992—dc20   89 – 27190
    ISBN 0-393-30656-9

Cover and chapter divider
illustrations by Huntley/Muir
Designed by Ellis/Esterson/Lackersteen
with Adam Hay

Picture Credits
Poltrona Frau 10
Rex Features 18, 22, 23, 28, 30, 46, 50,
53, 84, 116, 130, 131, 134, 135, 138, 143,
146, 152
Wilson 31
Hill Knowlton 37
Parfums Paloma Picasso 40, 41
Pepsi Cola 56
Pierre Cardin 63
Giorgio Armani 66, 71
Ralph Lauren/Polo Bruce Weber 78
Phil Sayer/*Blueprint* 90
Alessi 91
Donald Trump 97
Johnson/Burgee 97
Steve Speller/*Blueprint* 98
David Banks/*Blueprint* 99
Sottsass Associati 108
Anthony Fawcett 117
Villa Zapu 121
Absolut Vodka 125
Parfum Salvador Dali 127

W. W. Norton & Company, Inc, 500 Fifth Avenue, New York, N.Y. 10110
W. W. Norton & Company, Ltd, 37 Great Russell Street, London WC1B 3NU

Printed by Printer Portuguesa, Mem Martins, Portugal

1 2 3 4 5 6 7 8 9 0

Deyan Sudjic was born in London in 1952, of Yugoslav parents. He was educated at Latymer Upper School, and the University of Edinburgh, where he graduated in architecture in 1976. Having qualified, he decided not to practise as an architect, 'on the grounds that it would spare the world from yet more leaky and mediocre buildings'.

For eight years he was architecture correspondent of *The Sunday Times*, before starting his own magazine, *Blueprint*, in 1983. He now writes for *The Times* about conspicuous consumption, and contributes to a variety of magazines.

His first book, *Cult Objects*, was published in 1985.

DEYAN SUDJIC

CULT HEROES

HOW TO BE FAMOUS FOR MORE THAN FIFTEEN MINUTES

W. W. NORTON & COMPANY
New York   London

INTRODUCTION

Ferdinand Alexander Porsche, the man who gave up designing for the family car business to launch a thousand wristwatches bearing his name

The man with the Louis Vuitton briefcase on his knee, up in seat 3A in Business Class, personifies a new order. It defines itself not by nationality or class, but by allegiance to a select group of heroes. Push back his sleeve, and notice the gunmetal watch on his wrist. Ferdinand Alexander Porsche's name is etched across the face. Look closely at his steely spectacles and you find a discreet set of initials, just forward of the hinge, belonging to a French couturier. Open his jacket, and you see a label paying homage to Giorgio Armani. He wears a cologne applied from a bottle on which the words Salvador Dali are prominently displayed.

He could be from East Coast America, Northern Italy, South-East England, or just about anywhere in between. The names he wears are familiar in any language, enshrined in local Valhallas, distributed throughout the world's smarter shopping streets, and pirated and counterfeited in the open air markets of Bangkok and Hong Kong. They owe their special resonance to the aura that surrounds certain endlessly reproduced images. The concentration of media attention on a handful of individuals is so relentless, and so powerful, that, whether they like it or not, they find themselves transformed into icons.

The basis of such fame need have little connection with talent or accomplishment, and is sometimes almost entirely to do with presentation. The phenomenon is a more elegant version of the graffiti epidemic on the New York and London undergrounds. But while teenage delinquents with spray cans risk life, limb, and substantial fines for the pleasure of watching their names go by, cult heroes are paid handsomely for the use of their names.

And it's not just the nomadic BMW-driving classes who fall for their charms. Fame has become the most valuable, the most sought after, and the most perishable of commodities. It is used to sell the most mundane products: sunglasses, kettles, petrol, perfumes, wristwatches, cars, jeans, credit cards, and houses. All of these products, and many others, are regularly put on the market embroidered with the name of a famous individual, promoted directly, if misleadingly, as 'their' products, or endorsed by them.

Provided it is capable of being translated from the specialist to the general audience, where an individual's fame comes from is less important than the fact that it exists. Once celebrity is firmly established it holds its value in a host of other, scarcely related areas. So Michael Graves, currently the most over-exposed architect in the world, has been able to move into the mass market using his name to sell kettles, and carrier bags for Bloomingdales. And Björn Borg after peaking in his tennis career began to build a new one in fashion. Roger Daltrey no longer sings for a living, but he is still paid by American Express to endorse its charge cards.

This remarkable state of affairs has come about through a combination of the conscious manipulation of the celebrity-hungry media and the economic need of manufacturers to create an identity, and an image of status and prestige, for their otherwise indistinguishable mass-produced wares.

All kinds of inanimate objects are now being presented as embodying the characteristics of the famous. There is a development company which sells condominiums in Georgia as 'Jack Nicklaus' homes. Salvador Dali – or perhaps more accurately his minders – collects regular royalties from the manufacturers of scent that bears his name. Pepsi Cola invests millions of dollars persuading Michael Jackson to endorse its product, even though he refuses to drink it. And Coca-Cola responds by hiring Boris Becker to fight back on its behalf, investing heavily in a tiny patch on the sleeve of his tennis shirt; invisible to the centre court crowds, but perfectly positioned for television close-ups. The point, according to one advertising industry observer, is that

Pepsi is selling itself as 'youth', while Coca-Cola has traditionally symbolized 'America'. In the absence of a top-ranking American player, Becker is the closest that the company can get to finding a tennis star personifying the all-American virtues.

It is perfectly clear why the manufacturers do this. The addition of the name of a successful fashion designer to a mass-produced t-shirt or pair of sunglasses allows them to command premium prices. For an entrepreneur trying to start a chain of luxury hotels, or a smallish cigarette manufacturer breaking into the international market, borrowing the prestige of a famous name can be a vital short cut to capturing their audience. Rather than spending the millions needed to win recognition for a new brand through years of heavy advertising and marketing, buying the name of the right celebrity can give a new product a chance to project the same image, and to share in its lustre immediately.

What is less clear is why millions of sceptical consumers suspend disbelief long enough to pay the premium these products command. Part of the explanation seems to lie in the changing relationship between consumers and mass-produced goods. Of course, we are all very well aware that shops are full of inanimate, machine-made objects, but emotionally we want them to be more. And we want to use our possessions to express our sense of individuality and identity. At the same time there is a yearning to belong, to be able to define yourself as one of a group of a particular kind of people. And it is in the definition of these groups that possessions which can express a personality have a role to play. The secret for a manufacturer is to choose the appropriate personality for the product he is offering, one which expresses the right message to his target audience, one that matches their aspirations.

In the stone age of celebrity, the qualities looked for by its paymasters were straightforward enough. Heroes were expected to project youth, good looks, fitness, and so on. Now that personalities can be used to convey far more complicated shades of meaning, even the unlikeliest individuals find themselves courted for their names. Ronald Reagan began his public career endorsing cigarettes and shirts when he still looked the picture of health. Now film stars and fashion designers put their names to motorcars, and pop stars are flattered to be asked to lend their names to training shoes.

The sheer quantities of cash involved in the marketing of famous names inevitably attract attention. But beyond the money, the cult of fame has changed the way that a lot of things work. When the rules governing international tennis are tinkered with to allow the payment of up to $5 million for a handful of top-ranking players simply to put in an appearance at the Grand Prix tournaments, the whole structure of the game is altered. The gap between the richer top seeds and the poorer second tier players widens, and becomes harder and harder to bridge. Just as the nature of the world art market is distorted when collectors buy works of art not for the intrinsic quality of the painting, but because of the status of the artist; or when bulk collectors like the Saatchis get bored with Sandro Chia, say, and unload their holdings.

These changes amount to something rather more fundamental than the shifting back and forth of large amounts of cash. Perhaps the nature of the change can be explained partly by the isolation and anonymity of life in the big cities. There is an apparent yearning for hero figures, for personalities who can give a face to a product, and an identity to an organization. To service that demand, a handful of individuals have moved beyond celebrity to become cult heroes. They have a presence, whether it is created artificially or not, which has a powerful economic role.

Once celebrities used to achieve fame in their own narrow fields, and were known only to their followers and enthusiasts. The new celebrities are drawn from the ranks of successful musicians, film stars, artists, designers, and sportsmen. Their fame has ensured that they now have more in common with each other than with their fellow professionals. These are the cult heroes who have achieved the exposure to make them famous far beyond their obvious limits. They have become brand names, as universally recognizable as Ford or Coca-Cola. They are part of the cast of a real-life international soap opera.

The qualities of the new cult heroes have very little in common with the virtues attributed to heroes in the past. Chivalry and modesty are conspicuous by their absence. But then the new breed are rarely presented as role models in the way that heroes once were. Today's cult hero is seen by the audience as a focus for the projection of their dreams, more than as a model for emulation.

The phenomenon is by no means limited to the mass market. High culture is also transfixed by celebrity, to the extent that art, music, and theatre depend on the prestige of a select group of internationally recognized stars in exactly the same way as the cinema does. And these individuals are in some cases acquiring mainstream celebrity status too.

In creating celebrity, talent is less important than the cosmetic skills of presentation. It is a process that can be seen clearly at work in the music business where anonymous hit-making factories routinely use technically skilled producers to create hugely successful records by manufacturing a famous 'performer' whose involvement is limited to the use of their name on the label, and face on the album cover. The star provides a shop window for the technicians and session men who are actually responsible for the music.

The same techniques are used to build a recognizable image for a fashion designer and a sportsman, and the exploitation of their fame runs on ever more similar lines. Royalty, too, has been transformed beyond recognition as it has been sucked into the celebrity system. Mark Phillips licences wristwatches, leather goods and bracelets – using tasteful horseshoe motifs. A Diana range of cosmetics or tights would have a strength that could eclipse Pierre Cardin. In fact, the media treat the Princess of Wales as if she had already signed up to star in soap opera, with disastrous implications for the future standing of the British monarchy.

Two different processes are at work. At one end of the spectrum there is a production line producing new heroes. The other side of the equation is the consumption and exploitation of the celebrities as they emerge. Inevitably there are casualties. Boy George monogrammed sheets would, at best, have been a risky venture, and anyway Angela Rippon was spectacularly unsuccessful in trying to convert her unexpected fame into a fortune by this method. Gloria Vanderbilt, famous for being famous from the day she was born, flogged her name to death, capitalizing on it for all she was worth, but, with chronic over-exposure, found herself with a wasting asset. Some fashion designers actually lose control of the commercial use of their names. Others, notably Ralph Lauren, are assiduous in guarding the image that they create for their products through the skilful and subtle use of pictures and advertising.

Celebrity will undoubtedly be the greatest growth industry of the 1990s. It's an economic necessity more than an individual achievement or accident, and is already being manufactured and exploited with all the scientific deliberation and calculating investment of a production-line technique. As a key to understanding how popular culture works, and the way in which the images we manufacture have become end products in themselves, getting to grips with the cult hero is essential.

CHAPTER ONE

THE CELEBRITY INDUSTRY

From child actress to sex siren, Liz Taylor personified the traditional Hollywood star. Full lips and improbable eyebrows became trademarks, and every carefully posed studio shot made the most of them

Remarkably, in the late twentieth century, celebrity has come to be as much of a primary product as steel or coal once were. With its alchemical power to turn the least promising of raw material into alluring and desirable artefacts, it may even become *the* primary product.

Fame's economic applications are limitless. It can be manufactured, and bought and sold. Greedy entrepreneurs milk it shamelessly. The silver-tongued professions of design, advertising, and public relations have flourished on burnishing and exploiting it. And, in turn, celebrity has transformed everything it has touched. It has taken unchallenged possession of every nook and cranny of television, and destroyed the old myth of gentlemanly good sportsmanship. It has turned newspapers into a branch of the entertainment industry and put Ronald Reagan in the White House.

The cult of celebrity was born when the infant Hollywood discovered, with the arrival of the first fan magazines around 1912, that stars, not writers or directors, sold tickets. Audiences weren't that interested by what went on behind the camera, and got easily bored by the technicalities of plot. But the enormously magnified faces of the stars that dominated the ever-larger cinema screens of the twenties and thirties were another matter. Their power and sheer size dissolved the boundaries between reality and fantasy. The big screen, its impact heightened by the fantastical architecture of the old cinemas, created stars. It produced an extraordinary sense of intimacy between the performer and spectators in the darkened auditorium.

The first cinema stars were like turbocharged versions of the old mythical heroes, personalities whose magnetism created a massive new audience for film. The power of celebrity turned out not to be limited to the screen. Fame became an end in itself, which, when skilfully cultivated, could exist independently of the medium in which it grew, and even from the personality on which it was originally focused.

The methods once employed to create and exploit film stars set the pattern for the way that fame is now being used in a lot of other areas, from hard-nosed business to winsome entertainment. Chaplin, Fairbanks, Pickford, and the rest acquired a cachet that made them famous all around the world. Their images became icons transcending any dramatic role in which they happened to find themselves. On the screen, they appealed directly to the audience over the heads of any intermediaries, harnessing films, or so they thought, to their individual personality cults. In fact, it was the stars who were the fodder for the audience's voracious appetite for celebrity. It wasn't the everyday Chaplin or Pickford who they projected but a carefully constructed cinematic image. Mary Pickford, for example, had to go on playing adolescent girls well into her thirties, and provoked a revolt from her fans when she finally cut the curls that had become her trademark. Once the real figure beneath the image started to surface, when Chaplin's outspokenness was deemed un-American, or Pickford went through a messy divorce, the audience was scandalized at this threat to their perception of the star.

Even in the far-off innocent days of Hollywood's youth, celebrity was manufactured with a relentlessness that had uncomfortable parallels with the totalitarian movements of the twenties and thirties. Publicists, agents, and lighting cameramen were more important than drama teachers in making stars. Stars were created with a combination of guile, imagination, and surgery.

Would-be stars went in for physical remoulds, had their smiles straightened, their bosoms hoisted, and their hair and eye colour adjusted. Dietrich and Crawford, among others, had their back teeth extracted in the pursuit of razor-sharp cheekbones. Not much has changed. Now it's Liz Taylor and Cher who are whispered to have had surgery to remove their lower ribs in search of a slender waistline to stave off the effect of the passing years.

Newcomers began their careers in the Hollywood of the 1920s by posing for a portfolio of still pictures, carefully photographed in situations that projected the right messages: blatant sexuality in the case of the women, virility that bordered on caricature for the men. Yachts, fast cars, night-clubs, horses, firesides, and uniforms were all important props at different points in the careers of stars of both sexes. This artifice wasn't just aimed at casting directors, but was targeted at the press too. The right coverage could give aspiring hopefuls the exposure they needed to become stars almost without them having to venture onto the screen at all.

The public versions of their private lives were just as painstakingly prefabricated as their airbrushed, endlessly rehearsed studio portraits. Age and background and even their names were adjusted as required. Girlfriends, and marriages, could be arranged for male stars such as Rock Hudson whose sexual inclinations lay in other directions. Stars who toed the line and did as their publicists told them would be protected by the studios. If they broke the rules they got themselves blacklisted like Fatty Arbuckle after his name got dragged into a sex scandal. Toeing the line meant being seen around town at the right parties, photographed in glamorous restaurants, and taken out for ritualized public outings by agents and press secretaries, in as formal a manner as a levée at the court of Versailles.

In the early days there had been a lot of ambiguity about the relative status of star and vehicle. Even after Hollywood conceded the star-billing, salaries, contracts, and fancy dressing rooms that put the actors far ahead of the rest of the pack, the studios held on to the whip hand. In the twenties the stars were still the

creatures of the medium. Their names could guarantee the success of the right kind of film, but without the exposure of starring roles they would quickly have been forgotten. Figures like Garbo, who managed to maintain control of her own image, were rare. But that balance has steadily shifted.

From Paul Newman, and the spaghetti sauce that bears his name, to Raquel Welch, one of the thousands of names on the Rolodex of a New York name-broker who charges up to $7,500 to arrange for a star to make a personal appearance at your cocktail party, today's stars manipulate their prestige into economic assets over which they exert direct – if not always well-judged – control.

The stars who really make the big time are more than simply celebrities. They have become cult heroes, modern icons, whose essence is conveyed by a single frozen image made unreal but curiously intense by its lack of context. Our idea of Marilyn Monroe, for example, is not that of a walking, talking, human being, but of a static figure forever poised over a Manhattan pavement grating in *Seven Year Itch*, her skirts whirling round her neck, her candyfloss hair moulded into baroque contours, her smile an unfocused glint. Constant repetition of that image has given it a resonance and power that has outlived Monroe herself. Ironically, the image was artificially fabricated. Subway draughts, as it happens, don't blow skirts up unaided. Billy Wilder had a technician with a wind machine under the grating to make sure that Monroe's skirt moved on cue.

Monroe's screen presence had taken over the real person, with an image that had little to do with the flesh and blood woman. But then the same process has transformed our perception of so many cult heroes. The Christ-like Ché Guevara of the posters, with the wispy beard, the moustache, and the beret is as far removed from reality as the Monroe image. The same is true of James Dean. The actor who died young in his blazing Porsche roadster and Dean

If it hadn't been for an untimely exit after releasing *Rebel Without a Cause* and *East of Eden* in 1955, James Dean would be in his late fifties now, and that receding hairline would have vanished altogether. Just like Dean, Monroe's abiding appeal to manufacturers pursuing the youth market lies in the fact that she never grew old.

the ageless star of *Rebel Without a Cause*, with the famous profile, the white t-shirt, and the leather jacket, have led entirely independent existences.

Monroe, Dean, Bogart, and others have become abstract images more powerful than the reality. The stars are dead, but their heroic images live on, more valuable than ever, put to work now as part of the nostalgia bandwagon that sells cars, jeans, and beer. But as the commercial rights for their exploitation are syndicated and brokered out of existence, their images steadily lose their lustre. The Holsten brewery went to the length of buying a clip from an early Monroe film, splicing in its own footage, and screening the results as a television commercial. Too much of this kind of thing, and Monroe will be remembered not as the strawberry blonde personification of bitter-sweet 1950s sexuality, but as a high-pressure beer saleswoman.

In the old Hollywood, the economic value of fame was a fleeting by-product of the star's main role on screen. That has now given way to a much more systematic exploitation of the commercial value of celebrity, both in and out of the film world. We no longer have sportsmen, or fashion designers, or artists who happen to be famous. Instead we have people who are simply famous for being famous.

To attain this position it is not enough to be at the top of some obscure field of endeavour. There's not much mileage in being a famous stock-car driver, or a birdwatcher, or a trainspotter when the rest of the world isn't interested. Cult heroes depend on the lasting fame that comes from being famous for the right things. The first stage in becoming one is a public performance of some kind, in an arena in which anonymous individuals are transformed into heroes by the right kind of exposure.

Suitably telegenic sports are a proven vehicle for the creation of

Once the most famous name in tennis, Lacoste has turned into the sportswear status symbol that all newcomers try to emulate

celebrity. So far it is golf and tennis that have proved the most successful in producing new stars because they give the camera the chance to follow a face.

In economic terms the two markets with real clout are Japan and America. Both countries happen to be crazy about golf, and are almost as enthusiastic about tennis, much in line with the rest of the western world. However, both regard cricket as a mysterious Anglo-Saxon eccentricity, so, despite the obvious glamour of such heroes as Viv Richards or Imran Khan, the game remains a limited attraction. Polo, despite the connotations of glamour, luxury, and even the royal attachment of Prince Charles's name to the sport, has yet to produce major stars, mainly because nobody has managed to devise a satisfactory means of televising it. The action is too rapid and too diffuse to make an impact on the TV screen, which has taken over from film as the primary engine behind stardom. So polo stars, celebrated though they may be in the narrow confines of their own world, have yet to make it in the big-time celebrity stakes. Skiing makes better television, but it presents problems for the would-be cult hero. The equipment makes even the champions unrecognizable. They turn into colourful graphic blurs. Their names may become famous and as valuable as those of retired stars like Jean-Claude Killy, but they have trouble making it outside the sport because nobody knows what they look like. Motor racing, where the car is the real star, has the same problem.

New categories of stardom are constantly emerging, thrown up by the voracious demand for fresh raw material, and by the envy of those doing well in the more obscure fields of endeavour for their more celebrated contemporaries. Novelists and scientists are just as likely to enjoy being recognized in restaurants as ice skaters and actors, and they are perfectly happy to take the advertising agencies' money to endorse the wares of computer companies and liquor manufacturers.

Artists and architects have been amongst the most recent recruits to the celebrity system. Artist celebrities such as Julian Schnabel organize their careers with the deliberate aim of being famous, an undertaking in which Schnabel was greatly helped by the bulk purchasing of his work by the Saatchis. High-profile collectors add a useful hint of notoriety, but what makes Schnabel a celebrity is his fondness for being photographed, gazing moodily at the camera, by magazines like *Vanity Fair*. That and his unshakeable, and constantly repeated, belief in his position in the artistic pantheon alongside Goya, Van Gogh, and Piero della Francesca. None of the latter, however, turned their attention to designing a clothes shop as Schnabel has.

Keith Haring has taken the whole grisly process a stage further. His vacuous graffiti art lends itself perfectly to the commissions he has had from advertising agencies to decorate vodka bottles, and to his own merchandising activities which include producing t-shirts, postcards, and badges.

There are celebrity cooks, too, who insist on marching out into their restaurants to converse with the customers. When chefs such as Anton Mosimann maintain their own private dining rooms for particularly favoured guests, what one eats is clearly secondary to who has overseen its preparation. It is no surprise that Mosimann was the first chef to sign up with super-agent Mark McCormack, whose octopus-like grip has established a stranglehold on sports stars, the media, and the licensing business. Not content with starting his own private dining club in which one room is sponsored by Gucci, Mosimann is also working on books and TV programmes, with, no doubt, ranges of Mosimann food mixers and kitchen knives to follow in a carefully planned sequence.

The oddest class of celebrities are the creatures of the media: the television announcers, the weather forecasters, and the actors

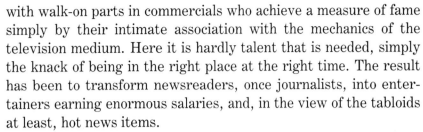

with walk-on parts in commercials who achieve a measure of fame simply by their intimate association with the mechanics of the television medium. Here it is hardly talent that is needed, simply the knack of being in the right place at the right time. The result has been to transform newsreaders, once journalists, into entertainers earning enormous salaries, and, in the view of the tabloids at least, hot news items.

The right kind of exposure is only one aspect of creating a cult hero. Manufacturing an identifiable image is equally important. Hollywood, first to discover the power of celebrity, is in turn now learning new tricks as film stars attempt to transform themselves from performers into branded goods. But the techniques originally pioneered by Hollywood are still in use. The methods it developed to recast personalities have been followed faithfully by the music business. Its image-building techniques, utilizing photography, fashion, and manufactured stage names, have followed Hollywood note for note. The first time around, in the late 1950s, with a straight face; the second, in the punk wave of the 1970s, with a knowing leer. That was when the Svengali-like figure of Malcolm McLaren turned a group of musical illiterates into the Sex Pistols. McLaren created the Sex Pistols by consciously turning upside down every received idea about how heroes should act and look. The Pistols were weedy and undernourished, they snarled, spat, and swore. They played around with all manner of suspect iconography, deviant sex, and swastikas. Anarchy became the basis for a corporate image. And, for a while, they were enormously successful, until the whole combustible mixture exploded.

Madonna, from the beginning, was as carefully designed an artefact as a Coke bottle or a Checker cab. The thrift shop chic she wore at the beginning of her career – ripped tights, lace, pork-pie hats and prominent crosses, selected for her by her dress

Who was that girl? Madonna went through a series of rapid fire image changes, from crucifixes to ripped lace tights, until she pinpointed Monroe as her heroine

consultant Marlene Stewart – amounted to a corporate identity. The image was tailored to be instantly recognizable, even when reproduced by the crudest of printing techniques, and visible at long distances – essential when performances are held in giant outdoor stadia. In the era of light shows and dry ice, Roger Daltrey's buckskin fringed jacket and Jimi Hendrix's trademark hat were enough. Madonna's characteristic use of underwear as outerwear, glitter-blonde hair dye, and bright red lipstick became a precise science. Trading on Marilyn Monroe's memory made her immediately identifiable, even as a doll-like figure, to people standing two football pitches away at the top of the stands at Wembley Stadium.

Michael Jackson, with his half-straightened hair looking like topiary, his accentuated, art-deco cheekbones, and curious sartorial mannerisms, notably his habitual single glove, is even more of a calculated creation. Jackson is a walking work of art who goes to totalitarian lengths to maintain control. He won't talk to the press. He does his best to buy up ownership of every photograph of himself. He insists musicians who work with him sign a legally enforceable agreement not to talk about him. Well he might. The power of his name has earned him an estimated $20 million from Pepsi Cola alone.

Jackson is all things to all men. Neither black nor white, neither masculine nor feminine, he looks like a bizarre blend of Napoleonic dandy and star trooper. Disturbingly, Jackson lists among his inspirations Liza Minelli, Diana Ross, and Peter Pan, a catholic enough collection to cover all the angles.

Once the star is airborne, the exploitation phase follows. The image that has been so carefully created is put to work. Initially the biggest problem is to make sure that the punters get the

message. Getting Mohammed Ali or Frank Bruno to smile at a TV camera and say yes, they eat X, is one way of doing it. Or it can operate at a more subliminal level: people agree to go to parties, artists are commissioned to design labels for beer or vodka bottles. Chrysler attempted to enlist the services of a musical cult hero. They wanted to borrow a slice of Bruce Springsteen's enormous prestige in America by offering him several million dollars to use the first few chords of 'Born in the USA' to open their new-model TV commercial campaign – and were turned down.

These are all different forms of the exploitation of celebrity. Few, however, are as mechanical as the way in which companies sponsoring sport use their stars as billboards. The most desirable properties are the tennis aces, signed up for lucrative financial deals, swapping their dignity for riches, and wardrobes that would make Ronald McDonald, the patron saint of hamburgers, blush.

Tennis wear has become a curious art form: every consideration of taste, style, and aesthetics has been sacrificed to the task of putting the sponsor's name across to the viewers at home as conspicuously as possible. Ironically, part of the problem is the very gentility of the tennis authorities, with their rules on what is and what is not acceptable dress. The All-England Lawn Tennis and Croquet Association, which runs Wimbledon, insists that players be dressed predominantly in white in all but the warm-up period, and that players who are not suitably dressed will be defaulted. It is a restriction that has only made things worse: the sponsors have become adept at getting the maximum exposure possible while keeping within the letter of the regulations. Hence the bizarre lengths to which they will go to plaster their stripes, symbols, and colours over every available square inch of cotton, towelling, and nylon.

Pat Cash, for example, is kitted out by an Italian sportswear firm, determined to let you know that its navy and pale blue checks are the only colours to wear this season. It's not just the arms of his shirt that are finished in checks; his shorts have a narrow line of blue piping around the pockets and inset bands of contrasting blue. Even his Davy Crockett-style headband has blue checks. Adidas, on the other hand, is attempting to glamorize the pre-printed typographic headband: to popularize the curious notion that walking around with somebody else's name wrapped around your forehead is an attractive idea. Some players carry a crop of Adidas logos swarming over their arms, chest, and, in case you had missed the point, sticking to their socks too, like a particularly persistent cloud of cluster flies.

It is not only the sports firms who use tennis players as walking advertisements. One cigarette company outrageously attempted to appeal to younger women smokers by turning Martina Navratilova into an orange and brown striped cigarette packet. Navratilova also ended up in the ludicrous position at one Wimbledon tournament of opting for a racket made by a company other than her sponsor's, and attempting to put the sponsoring company's logo on it.

Cyclists and motor racing drivers manage to look glamorous covered from head to foot in brand names, perhaps because there are fewer misguided attempts to impose gentility on them by keeping logos to a minimum size. Professional cycling kit – wet-look, skin-tight, long shorts, and heraldic jerseys – has turned into desirable street fashion. And in motor racing completely new garments have been invented, expressly to display as many logos as possible – for example, the peaked cap with the huge crown, handy for displaying huge bold type but hardly essential under your helmet at the wheel of the car.

Endorsements like these are the primitive phase of celebrity exploitation. It's simple minded and not very sophisticated, whether it's Frederick Forsyth telling the world about his Rolex, or Tama Janowitz jumping on tables to sell alcohol. In the long run it's not likely to do either of them much good. A much bigger earner is the transformation of a personality into a brand name selling products in which the star has a direct stake. Stars who do this are attempting to capitalize on the value of their own names, not to add glamour to those of their sponsors. The pioneers of this sort of licensing came from the fashion industry, where names have long been used to transform simple garments into desirable means of signifying status.

In the old days sports careers were brief. Now they last longer, not always with much dignity. Sports stars still have a continuing tendency to suffer from rapid burn-out. Self-destructive personalities such as George Best and Boy George have been more common in sport and music than stable business brains such as Giorgio Armani or Ferdinand Alexander Porsche, who have the inclination and ability to plan their careers.

The financially successful star has to have the staying power and the emotional equilibrium not to buckle under the pressure of constant recognition and attention. The long-term financially successful stars are the ones who do not throw tantrums or tennis rackets, who do not assault photographers, but who instead are able to maintain an even keel in front of the cameras, to be courteous and polite, to talk the language of chat shows. Above all, they must not sell themselves at too cheap a price. Unlike the journalist and entertainer Angela Rippon, they must have the common sense to realize that offering to put their names to a range of dolls is not going to do their long-term image any good, just as film stars have to know which parts to turn down, or the designer needs to know which chair commission to reject if he is not to become stale and over-exposed.

The new techniques used by aspiring cult heroes from diverse fields are the same. Duran Duran, the winsome but hugely successful musicians, were amongst the first to set the new pattern. They hired Malcolm Garrett as a resident graphic designer to work not just on their record covers, but on their posters, brochures, programmes, and on an astonishing variety of merchandise, from batteries to board games, that carried their name. 'I always treated Duran Duran as a corporation. I did the sleeve for their first single as though they were an airline company,' says Garrett. 'We tried to develop a corporate identity that was constantly updatable and renewable.'

Garrett devised the Duran Duran logotype that allowed them to register the name as a trademark, even though they had borrowed it from Roger Vadim's *Barbarella*. A logo and £20,000 in legal fees gave them worldwide control of the name. It then became the principal asset of the highly successful merchandise unit that made up part of the group's full-time establishment, run by a controller responsible for stamping out pirating, and negotiating licensing deals. What made Duran Duran products different from the countless cheap and nasty novelties that carried the Beatles name, for example, was that the group either sold designs for each specific licensed product, or insisted on design approval for all merchandise.

Fashion names such as Jean-Paul Gaultier or Christian Lacroix could hardly do more, and often do rather less, to control the way their names are used by some of their farther-flung licensees. The handkerchief departments of smarter Tokyo department stores are full of merchandised products bearing such names which have never even been seen by their alleged creators.

If business needs stars to sell its products, so do newspapers. And newspapers have the power to help to create the stars. In the early days of Hollywood, the press quickly found it was able to construct a world of its own around celebrity, peopled with a fluctuating cast of characters who kept their pages full of sensational melodrama. Their comings and goings quickly spilled out of the entertainment and gossip columns and onto the front pages, and the boundary between on- and off-screen activities vanished. Ever since, the relationship between the famous and the fame makers has been intimate and mutually profitable. Press and television play a vital role in making film stars famous, thereby helping to sell more tickets. And, in turn, by covering the stars that they have helped create, they have sold more newspapers.

The relationship between stardom and the press in general has proved to be a highly unstable one. Discovering feet of clay quickly turned out to be more likely to boost circulation than building heroes up. Look at the way that the British tabloids turned, snapping and yowling, to depict the Princess of Wales as an empty-headed Sloane, after years of fawningly presenting her as personifying all the virtues of a madonna. The same tabloids handed out similar treatment to the cricketer Ian Botham. Rupert Murdoch's *Sun*, in particular, shifted with astonishing speed from employing Botham to put his name to a regular column for the paper to assigning a full-time reporter to keeping an eye on his behaviour. In the process, the loud-mouthed Botham went from outspoken but lovable man of the people to personification of all that's unacceptably yobbish about Britain, before reappearing as a columnist for the *Sun*'s stablemate, *Today*.

Interdependence quickly breaks down – a process speeded up by the competitive nature of the press system. Newspapers and magazines need exclusives. They need above all to go on discovering fresh new faces if they are not going to look stale. The stars, and those who employ them, want maximum coverage, and the two forces collide, resulting in the phenomenon which puts Madonna on the cover of every glossy magazine in the world in the same week, and then sees the same magazines drop her as over-exposed shortly afterwards.

Access to celebrities is carefully controlled by their managers. The grander public relations consultants bristle fiercely if journalists so much as consider calling their clients directly. They allocate exclusives in bite-size slivers, hence the extraordinary phenomenon of the shared exclusive. In the same week, Jackie Collins is to be found holding forth in an 3000-word interview on *The Guardian* women's page, talking about a room of her own to the *Evening Standard*, selecting her favourite restaurant for the *Sunday Express* – all events related entirely to the fact that she is about to publish a new book. Remarkably, the browbeaten hacks, desperate not to be cut off from their access to the supply of celebrity, co-operate. The burgeoning public relations business exists to provide reasons, spurious or otherwise, for the press to cover their clients. The more sophisticated practitioners have become highly skilled at providing magazines, newspapers, and TV stations with pegs: a convenient opening, a photo opportunity, mixed with a little judicious bribery – a transatlantic flight for an exclusive interview in America, perhaps.

The way that journalism is structured makes their task easier. The press has a tendency to believe that news only exists when somebody else has covered a story first. Rather than follow their own instincts, editors look for reassurance. When journalistic impulses do occasionally reassert themselves, it is to undermine rivals, to expose the shortcomings of their tame celebrities, or, more often, to try to spoil their scoops by lifting exclusive pictures or stories and adopting them as their own.

Some stars take the view that they don't need the press. There are those, such as Robert de Niro, who decide not to speak to them at all, an approach which is not without promise for media coverage. Nothing is so tantalizing, after all, as studied

Michael Jackson is the best-selling recording star of all time, but there are signs that the commercial appeal of his name is slipping. Pepsi's British distributors voiced doubts about showing Jackson TV commercials for the product, and his licensing deal with Warren Hirsch, king of the designer jeans business, ended in tears

indifference. Many stars claim to guard their privacy, yet always ensure that the paparazzi are tipped off to record their entrances and exits from star-watching restaurants like Langan's Brasserie or Mr Chow's. Raw celebrity needs an arena for its display. Smart restaurants and bars fit the bill, and stars are happy to use the despised press to keep their profile high.

It is a point demonstrated by Peter J. Stringfellow, proprietor of the eponymous London and New York discotheques, when he issued a circular letter, signing himself 'Yours sincerely, and your friend', which began with the words 'Dear celebrity member'. It went on: 'Please excuse me for not writing personally, but I am sending this letter to all of my celebrity members. It has to be said that recently press photographers have overdone the String-fellow bit, so much so in fact that it has made a lot of my celebrity members uncomfortable. So the new policy is that press photographers will not be allowed into Stringfellows on social evenings except when we have PR promotional activities, which of course are a different matter altogether, i.e. Björn Borg's recent toiletry launch.'

The subjects covered by the press define the identity that the medium chooses, consciously or unconsciously, to project. Photographs of the British royal family have now come to indicate a down-market paper or magazine, courting a mass circulation audience, so that those seeking a different type of reader avoid royal 'news' and pictures as much as possible.

As the world gets used to the manufacture and consumption of celebrity, the techniques deployed by the famous, the would-be famous, and those who use them, become more and more sophisticated. But so does the response of the audience. The longevity of stars gets shorter all the time. The true cult heroes retain their power and attraction, but admission to their ranks becomes ever more difficult.

CHAPTER TWO

A QUESTION OF IDENTITY

Paloma Picasso sells individuality: her powerful profile is a far cry from the conventional celluloid good looks of the models normally hired for perfume ads. But it is L'Oreal, the biggest perfume company of them all, which calls the shots

From the window of an optician's shop in the heart of fashionable London, Paloma Picasso stares out frostily at passing shoppers. Her chin is propped on her thumb. Her leather-gloved and bejewelled forefinger points skyward, buttressing her spectacular cheekbones. The flecks of light reflected in her impossibly scarlet lips and in her sleek black mane of hair give her the slick gloss of a cherished limousine. The same glossy lips curl at apparently identical, affluent shoppers when they venture into range of the fallout from the waterfall in the Trump Tower atrium in New York, across the marble-floored shopping malls of Hong Kong Central, and through the Duty Free supermarket at Dubai airport.

Self-possessed, voluptuous, and expensive, her image is reproduced on stout laminated cardboard in thousands of shop windows, and repeated endlessly in the glossy magazines. Despite her expression of well-bred disdain, her image is in the shop to sell spectacles. Not just any spectacles, of course, but Paloma Picasso spectacles. And in the magazines she sells the perfume that is also blessed with her signature, with a similar photograph. Without the Picasso name, and the sullen photograph of its curiously spectacle-free, but no doubt fragrant, owner, what would these products be? A plastic-coated set of wire-reinforced spectacle frames, and a bottle of scented water laced with alcohol. Add the carefully polished Picasso image, and at once they take on a distinctively different identity. They become desirable products that mean something special to their purchasers, or so Picasso's licensees hope, anyway.

This is not some vulgar commercial transaction, they imply, but a marriage made in heaven. 'It truly is my perfume. Like everything I create and everything with which I surround myself, it embodies my tastes, my passions, and my artistic choices,' gush Paloma and her copywriters. And to help get the message across, the company engraves her signature on the bottle in what it describes unblushingly as the 'finest gold'.

Paloma, it maintains with a straight face, 'directed each stage of the creation, the bottles, the cases, and the perfume itself. We can guess the potency of the scent's personality from its wrapping alone.' It is a claim that sits a little uncomfortably with the reality behind Picasso's sleek image. For, in perfume terms at least, her name belongs to L'Oreal, the $4 billion cosmetics company, the largest in the world, which also markets Lauren and Vanderbilt fragrances. It's a giant multinational which does most of its business in the supermarkets and which began back in 1907 when Eugene Schueller started boiling up hair dye in his Paris flat.

That the transformation of spectacle frames and scent bottles works so effectively does not say much for the sceptical hard-headedness of the consumer who buys them. It is difficult to argue about how much value for money the Picasso name represents from the point of view of consumerism. *Which?* magazine, if it tackled it, would have to end up investigating whether Picasso represents better or worse value than Elizabeth Taylor or Giorgio Armani on a more-blobs-the-better basis. Certainly Picasso looks to be the classiest, if not the most expensive, of the trio, despite the fact that her perfume comes in a bottle that looks like a ground-glass fried egg. Liz Taylor's competing advertisement, on the other hand, though it boasts a photograph, prominently credited to Norman Parkinson, of a newly slenderized Taylor decked with several million dollars' worth of diamonds, is let down by a bottle that looks like the radiator mascot of a particularly ostentatious cod-1930s sports car. But then Taylor – or rather Parfums International Inc. – is presumably looking for an older market: one which needs its ego more heavily massaged than Paloma Picasso's. One brand croaks 'mature but sexy', the other whispers 'sexy but sophisticated'.

Consumerist logic has never been much of an issue in the purchase of such essentially escapist products as perfume. But the curious thing about the present boom in the sale of celebrity artefacts is that they are spreading into areas that were once simply utilitarian, but which now present an opportunity for creating a product that carries a message – for example, bathrobes, mineral water, and sunglasses. This is all in the interests of the manufacturers, because it gives them a chance to engineer a suspension of disbelief over the price tag. But it also taps a genuine desire to make everyday objects and artefacts that offer more than simple utility.

Paloma Picasso is an obligingly non-specific sort of celebrity. She is famous for nothing in particular. There has been no Picasso film career, she is not a sports champion, she has not written a best-seller, or starred in a TV series. If she is famous for anything apart from being Paloma Picasso, it is for being Pablo Picasso's daughter. And it is that fact that allows her to be all things to all consumers. Manufacturers can be confident that the Picasso name is not going to offend people who don't like sport, or put off those who think that film stars are a bit too obvious. And her name is curiously free of any national inflection: not quite American, not quite European, but equally recognizable on both sides of the Atlantic. It's the kind of celebrity that could have been created in the test tube, precisely engineered for maximum market appeal, while retaining vaguely cultural overtones. Putting the Picasso name on your product is certainly enough to help it to stand out from the anonymous herd.

As names go, Paloma Picasso's has a curious power. It rolls off the tongue sonorously, sugar-coated with prestige. So Pablo himself, owner of the name to end all names, who even in his own lifetime could turn walls and tablecloths into works of art simply by signing them, may be unavailable. But the almost equally resonant Paloma is yours for the asking, provided the price is right. And there is more. The icing on the culture cake is the aura of life in the fast lane – Concorde tickets, haute couture, social accept-ability, and an abundance of money – which the striking Ms Picasso projects. Above all there are those photogenic cheekbones, and the lip-curling sneer. It is exactly these qualities that Picasso's licensees are looking for. The Picasso name is their passport to projecting an unambiguous message about their products.

It's not the physical differences between Picasso and Porsche or Oldfield glasses that matter. The designer's room for manoeuvre is limited: the differences between basic form, engineering, and so on are close enough, from one brand to another, to be on the point of being invisible. What the licensee is paying for is not Paloma Picasso's design skills, but the chance to tap into a specific group of people, those who define themselves consciously or unconsciously by their possessions. These are the individuals who tell the world the kind of people they are, or want to be, by the things that they own. People see themselves as a Paloma Picasso, or an Issey Miyake, or an F.A. Porsche. And when they have discovered the group that they identify with, they tend to go for the whole kit: the clothes, the perfume, even the eyewear, as it is called.

Identifying a product so firmly with a given hero can be a means of reassuring the socially anxious about the impression they are making. It can be used for role-playing games, chopping and chang-ing identities. Nor does the name necessarily have to be flaunted publicly. Even when the outside world has no way of knowing about it, it can still keep the consumer happy. Just how valuable the control of the right names has become can be seen in the unseemly war that raged within the ranks of the Gucci family when Paolo Gucci broke with his father, and the rest of his family, and went to court to protect his right to sell products under his own name. The family feud sparked off a bitter board-room struggle, which on one occasion at least drew real blood, when the rest of the Guccis tried to stop him. There was even talk of Paolo Gucci jeans at one point. A contradiction in terms, or so the Gucci public relations department would have us believe, as they concentrate instead on implying that Guccis have been saddlemakers by appointment to the Florentine gentry since the days of the Medicis.

Names have become so valuable because there are not that many about that can work the magic of the Picassos or the Guccis, and because their exploitation has become an increasingly important part of the way that the economy works. The longer they have been around, the more they carry the accumulated patina of prestige that can only be accrued gradually, carefully, or with enormous expenditure.

When Ford sold its first mass-produced cars, and when Braun produced its record players, these things were in themselves such exceptional developments that they attracted an eager audience: just like the first Walkman, or the first colour TV set. But innovation at this level gets to be difficult, and hugely expensive. Within a given price range most products are essentially the same, whatever company sells them. And the innovating companies have less and less time to exploit the advantages of being first.

Marketing tacticians now create an image for their products which flatters their audience into buying them. But there is a need for a level of taste and discretion if the gap between image and product is not to become too wide.

The reason why named products have a lasting appeal often comes down to trust. If you like and admire a designer's skill with making trousers then you are more inclined to accept that he can transfer that to something quite unrelated – sunglasses, perhaps – even though he or she has had nothing to do with their design or making. The transference can be achieved with quite humble products – t-shirts, socks, underwear – with the effect that the added prestige persuades people to pay a premium.

45

Diamonds are still a girl's best friend – even after a spell in the Betty Ford Clinic. Taylor's perfume, Passion, comes in a glitzy bottle that deliberately recalls her fondness for precious stones

Sometimes the association with a famous name is made purely for the purpose of creating a better image. The point is not to make money in the short term, but to invest in the future. Everybody has heard of the British glass manufacturer Pilkington, but few have heard of its optical glass division. So, to enhance its image, the company hired Bruce Oldfield to put his name to a new range of eyewear. This has resulted in a brisk market for premium eyewear for Oldfield, and the enhancement of the Pilkington name, marking its entry into consumer goods; no bad idea when its patents for money-spinning industrial products are beginning to run out. The Mouton Rothschild vineyard, in its lengthy battle to be accepted as a *premier cru*, waged a similar campaign. It invested in the image of its brand with a succession of specially commissioned labels from famous artists; the implication being that it was part of the country's national heritage.

As long as the appetite for products that project a personality continues, then the cult of celebrity will go on exercising the talent and ingenuity of the masters of marketing and design. And personalities will need to exercise great care in their attempts to transform themselves into brand names, for even cult heroes have to go on living up to the message if they are to go on working. Their status is dependent on public perceptions.

Modern cult heroes seldom conform to traditional ideas of heroism. We live in a period in which notoriety can be seen as just as desirable. Even individuals accused of murder have the potential for celebrity status. EastEnders, Britain's best-rated soap, has a star who is a convicted murderer, while in America Klaus von Bülow, after being acquitted of murder at his trial, was to be seen posed in the glamour-soaked pages of *Vanity Fair*, photographed by Helmut Newton: not a hero exactly, but certainly a celebrity. Bülow is not yet in demand for licensing his name for scent, but one day, perhaps.

47

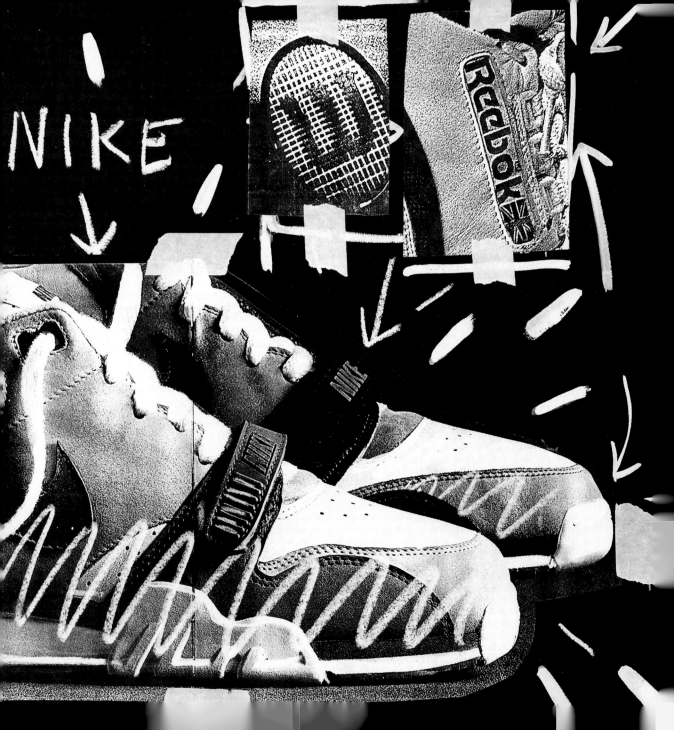

CHAPTER THREE

THE PRICE
OF FAME

Is he serious? Borg's hairy and humourless Centre Court image hardly seemed to promise a career as a fashion arbiter

Björn Borg doesn't want to be forgotten. In his low-key Swedish way, he's desperate not to go the same route as Ilie Nastase, Arthur Ashe, or any of the other no-longer-big names of the tennis world.

In his days on the Centre Court, they used to call him the ice man, primarily because, unlike the tantrum-throwing players of his generation, he wasn't interested in hurling his racket around, or shouting at umpires. His most rebellious gesture was to strap on a headband that scrunched his hair up and made him look like a turnip.

For a while, it seemed as if Borg's primary aim in life was to be remembered for making a great exit. In 1980, he went to five sets at Wimbledon with the upstart McEnroe, winning the fourth by eighteen games to sixteen, his fifth Wimbledon victory in a row. The next year, minutes after McEnroe had finally beaten him, Borg slipped away. Cool as ever, he headed for Heathrow in a taxi, ending a ten-year career that had made him more than $10 million in prize money, without saying a word. Now, at thirty-one, his Viking locks cropped, Borg's face, with its Munster forehead and raw-boned features, has taken on the look of a freshly scrubbed potato. He has discarded tennis whites, shorts, and headbands for baggy suits that flap in the wind from his lanky frame. A motorway pile-up of stripes cascades up and down his suit, dazzles over his shirt, and shrieks in fright-stripe diagonals across his tie.

This is the new Borg, bent on transferring the value of the celebrity he acquired as a sportsman to a new and vastly more lucrative career – that of licensing his name. Borg's professional signature seems to have been heavily influenced by the carefully practised scrawl of starlets who leave names like Toni or Jacqui smeared across bathroom mirrors in pink lipstick. It is already appearing on luggage, men's clothes, and cosmetics. On the Björn

51

Borg Worldwide collection of luggage, it has been silkscreened across shocking purple and yellow reinforced nylon fabric in letters as big as your arm, presumably to ensure that even the most myopic of passers-by will not fail to get the message. It is rather more discreetly in evidence on his menswear range: would-be high fashion produced by the Björn Borg Design Group, which is embellished by a comparatively low-key logo, a star abstracted out of Borg's initials.

The impact of sport on fashion has been enormous, to the point where the high streets are full of sports shops selling tracksuits and singlets to an audience that would never dream of participating in anything so strenuous as athletics. Even running shoes are now produced in sizes suitable for babes in arms. But jumping from sport into mainstream fashion is a difficult manoeuvre and Borg may yet come unstuck. Successful sports businessmen have so far kept pretty close to their roots. Jack Nicklaus with his Nicklaus golf courses, and his Nicklaus time-share housing developments, has been the most ambitious of them.

Now nearing fifty, he earned $5 million at the peak of his golf career, a figure that pales into insignificance beside the money he has made from the assiduous exploitation of his name. His Golden Bear Corporation, which makes most of its money designing golf courses at fees of up to $1 million each, has ninety-two employees. Nicklaus's other activities have not been so successful. He lost $3 million on the St Andrews Golf Club at Hastings on Hudson, New York, where he not only designed the course, but invested his own money in the development. The Nicklaus restaurant chain didn't prosper either. But he is still selling housing plots on Jack Nicklaus residential communities for $250,000 each. And in Japan $212 million worth of Nicklaus merchandise, from health food to cosmetics, was sold in the last year by his licensee Kosugi Sangyo.

The ever-increasing amount of money involved in sport has had the effect of enhancing the names associated with it, in just the same way that the escalating value of contemporary art has improved the status of artists. In the USA, sports sponsorship totalled $1.35 billion in 1987, with Boris Becker, who made $5 million out of Coca-Cola and Polaroid, at the top of the tree, closely followed by Greg Norman, who made $4 million from Reebok and Epson.

Even off the court Borg projects all the glamour of a youth club disco, with a dress sense to match

At Wimbledon, prize money has leapt up from £26,000 in 1968, when it was first introduced, to £2.6 million in 1988. And in motor racing, sewing a patch on the right pair of overalls will cost a sponsor £250,000. Nevertheless, sports heroes, like the high-earning American baseball and football players, have mostly kept their licensing deals to straight endorsements.

Now Borg wants to change all that. He is cutting all but the most vestigial links with his sporting origins – the Borg cologne is called 6–0 – and straining to become more than just a tennis player who happens to be famous. By being famous for being Björn Borg he has a chance of turning his fame into a much bigger economic asset than his sports earnings could ever have amounted to. Already his over-excitable agent is talking about an annual turnover of $50 to $100 million a year in Borg products in the early 1990s. It's the type of figure plucked out of a hat with such monotonous regularity by the people who handle celebrities that you can't help but treat it with a little suspicion. Michael Jackson's former licensing agent Warren Hirsch used exactly the same numbers when talking about the market for Jackson products.

But then marketing men always like to add as many noughts to their figures as they dare. The $100 million, if Borg gets it, would represent total sales for every company in the world selling Borg-licensed merchandise. His share of that in royalties would vary between five and ten percent, depending on the type of product, representing a maximum of $10 million a year. From that money would have to be deducted his agent's fee – it could be as much as forty percent – and the costs of running the Borg studio.

After the golden age of Fred Perry, Henri Lacoste, and Arnold Palmer, with their apparently Olympian detachment from grubby commerce and their Chariots of Fairisle good sportsmanship, today's sports heroes have to contend with the sleaze that has caught up with sport. Hooliganism is now as routine around the pitch as drug taking is in the changing room. Presenting athletes as the great white hopes they used to be when the amateur enjoyed an edge of prestige over grubby professionals who only did it for the money is getting more difficult. Rock stars are supposed to behave badly, but the loutish behaviour of so many sports names cuts across the sporting myths established by the old amateur tradition.

None of this does much for the earning power of sports stars. Even cricket is tainted, and the lure of fame and fortune has changed not just the public perception of the players, but the game itself. Cricket is played to special rules at one-day events, seen as more lucrative in sponsorship terms, but, by purists at least, as truncating the classic game to a stunted travesty.

Ian Botham might once have done pretty well out of selling breakfast cereals on television, but these days he is limited to promoting low-alcohol beer. Footballers have a decidedly limited appeal because of the down-market image of the game. Skiing still offers a more glamorous edge, partly because it takes place in exotic locations, and participation is costly. Tennis is midway between the two: attracting huge audiences but not yet too disrupted by hooligan elements.

When he was still playing, Borg managed to steer clear of the problems with the press that McEnroe and even Connors faced. It was a reasonable start for a full-time career as a hero, if a little colourless. His problem now is where to pitch his commercial image in stylistic terms. Former tennis players, especially Swedish former tennis players like Borg, with a reputation for implacable efficiency rather than stylistic flair, are going to have trouble being taken seriously alongside such fashion heroes as Armani and Yamamoto. Instead, Borg seems to be concentrating on the pink-faced, flaxen-haired Scandinavian kids, who, when they eventually grow out of their Benetton and Esprit, start looking around for casual suits.

Borg seems to be trying to offer the classless Eurolook. His clothes project the same kind of feeling you get from listening to Italian would-be rock stars singing in English and aiming at a Belgian audience; a little bland, certainly inoffensive, and, with the benefit of the Borg name, likely to convince the easily impressionable that they are getting something special. But to sustain himself in the fashion world, he is going to have to do more than rely on the power of his name. Borg will have to create for himself the kind of visual image that Ralph Lauren and Calvin Klein have perfected if he is going to last. Michael Jackson has his concerts, videos, and records to back up his name. Cardin has the Paris collections. But with his championship days over, Borg has little more than rapidly fading memories of his past glories to rely on.

Assuming responsibility for the way the products look, allows celebrities, or their managers, to exercise more control over products with which their names are being associated. Cheap and nasty goods reflect badly on the value of the name. And so does commercial failure. Care is needed in choosing which firms to license – a care which is tempered by the knowledge that unauthorized use is always a strong possibility.

Yet subtlety and finesse are hardly the strong points of many of the denizens of the fame business. Agents have been known to produce mail shots touting their clients and Joan Collins, for one,

Bad for you, but lucrative. The word is that Michael Jackson won't drink Pepsi on health grounds, but Pepsi calculates that the right picture is worth several million dollars. Linking Jackson with its logo counts for much more than the small print of the message

had her charms hawked around in this way. This is, of course, potentially counterproductive: the most valuable names are the ones that manufacturers approach, rather than the ones that come out looking for business.

Warren Hirsch, the man who launched Gloria Vanderbilt's name on a million pairs of jeans, went to the lengths of buying a double page spread in *Women's Wear Daily*, declaring Michael Jackson's name available for licensing. 'Put the most powerful name in American entertainment to work for you,' he barked. 'If you doubt the commercial power of Michael Jackson's name, look at his record of hits and upcoming events. All work together to sell your product,' enthused Hirsch before presenting Jackson's entire career to date as an exercise in marketing. Sales of eight million copies of the 'Off the Wall' album and thirty-eight million copies of 'Thriller' were simply a curtain-raiser to 'helping Pepsi Cola to record the largest gross sales in their history'. In case the punters lacked the imagination to see what they could do with the asset of the Jackson name behind them, Hirsch offered a few suggestions of his own: lunch buckets, headwear, bumper stickers, luggage, electronics, bicycles; all of them, apparently, the kind of products that 'megastar Michael Jackson's name could send through the roof'.

In the summer of 1988 Hirsch's relationship with Jackson had come to an end, with profits well short of the roof. Hirsch quickly went into partnership with Gloria Vanderbilt for a come-back on the jeans front. 'We'd have done better with a little more co-operation. The Jackson clothes sold OK when he was on tour, but when he stopped, they just died,' confided a sadder, wiser Hirsch. Nevertheless, Jackson has done remarkably well from his non-endorsement endorsement of Pepsi. His latest and most lucrative deal was for $15 million, part of the company's war with Coca-Cola. According to *Rolling Stone*, his henchmen Frank Dileo and

John Branca negotiated Jackson's second deal with Pepsi's president, Roger Enrico, in March 1986. Jackson collected a $15 million advance, which allowed Pepsi to put its logo on the programmes for the proposed 1987 Michael Jackson world tour – his last, according to manager Dileo – and to use him in two commercials for the company.

Branca had already negotiated similar, if smaller, deals for Elton John, Mick Jagger, and Miami Vice's Don Johnson, among others, but this was his biggest coup and won him a $120,000 Rolls Silver Spur as a bonus from Jackson. The Pepsi money was paid in advance, but Jackson didn't deliver on schedule. The tour did not, in fact, take place until 1988. The whole campaign had been designed to coincide with the release of what was meant to be the best-selling record album in the history of the world: 'Bad'. Jackson was talking about selling 100 million copies before he had even started work on it. In the event, it took so long to make that Pepsi were stuck without a campaign in 1987, and had to bring in David Bowie and Tina Turner as stop-gaps.

The American lawyer Mark McCormack has played a crucial part in creating a new kind of business-conscious celebrity. McCormack built his empire on a friendship with the golfer Arnold Palmer. Back in the early 1960s, at a time when sportsmen didn't expect to make a living from their sports, McCormack quickly made Palmer into a millionaire by acting like a Hollywood agent. Palmer passed the message on to friends like Jack Nicklaus and Gary Player who became clients too, and so McCormack grew into the International Management Group, a business with twenty offices around the world, and 450 employees, which earned $400 million in 1987. IMG's clients include 350 athletes, along with fashion designers, TV commentators, the Pope, and even a town: St Moritz.

McCormack is more than an agent for the stars and an expert

at licensing their names. He has transformed the shape of sport around the world. He has his foot planted firmly on the soft underbelly of the whole system. He acts for the players, and he advises the commercial sponsors on how to spend their money to make the greatest impact. When the sports associations ran out of events to sell to the queue of would-be sponsors, McCormack created a string of brand new championships out of thin air. There are scores of European golfing events created by McCormack, primarily in the interests of giving his clients the exposure they want. McCormack now even appears as a TV commentator himself. Turn on a TV set to watch the Fiat Pro-Am Snooker Pool tournament and you will see an event dreamed up by McCormack, sold by McCormack to the networks, staged in St Moritz, the company town, and commentated on by another McCormack client, wearing St Moritz-licensed sunglasses designed by yet another McCormack associate. According to the McCormack empire, 'St Moritz can expect to make rather more than the average golf star for its name, but rather less than a major tennis player.'

McCormack's IMG group counts on getting an initial down-payment from the manufacturer of one year's predicted revenues, subject to a minimum of perhaps $100,000, with annual royalty payments of anything up to ten percent of the wholesale price of the products with the star's name on them. McCormack's power as an agent has enabled him to push his share of clients' earnings higher and higher, up to a reputed forty percent in some cases. In fact, in the case of St Moritz, the resort is guaranteeing McCormack a minimum $500,000 for his help in selling the name to mineral-water bottlers, cosmetics companies, the German optician's union (for sunglasses), and even a Swiss furniture company who are planning to produce the St Moritz chair.

There are those who believe that McCormack is selling Switzerland's snootiest ski resort too cheaply: he licensed St Moritz to a champagne company, who use the name on a plebian non-vintage bottle.

The earning power of a name varies enormously. Music figures have been known to ask for, and get, thirty percent and more of the revenue from products they license, a state of affairs that they can help to engineer by retaining the copyright of all their photographs, giving their image a scarcity value.

Fashion names have been making big money for the last decade or so. Ralph Lauren is reckoned to be the richest of all the American fashion names. Rag trade insiders reckon he is worth $300 million. During 1987 he sold 625 million dollars' worth of Lauren branded goods, from furniture to fragrance.

Lauren's directly owned company, Polo/Ralph Lauren, produces the high-price menswear range and handles all the licensing deals. Bidermann Industries is his women's licensee, and Cosmair, the L'Oreal subsidiary that sells his men's and women's fragrances, sells $125 million worth of unguents of all kinds a year, netting Lauren perhaps ten percent of that sum.

Lauren's nearest rival, Calvin Klein, bought up his own loss-making licensee Puritan Fashions Corp. in 1983, when the designer jeans market collapsed. In 1984 Klein revealed that he had earned a grand total of $1,234,700 that year.

Owners of desirable names are in a financially secure position: they have no need to invest money themselves to get a steady return. If things go well all they will be called on for is a specified number of personal appearances. However, even the most valuable names are too fragile to leave to the mercies of unrestrained licensing. Short-term greed tends to win out over careful husbanding of the image of a name. The risks, but also the potential rewards, are higher when the stars themselves invest in their

Dressed to kill: Pierre Cardin was the first of the fashion names to lend his prestige to the cigarette industry. Yves St Laurent has followed in his footsteps

names. It provides them with a greater measure of control over their exploitation.

Pierre Cardin has one of the most valuable names in the world. In 1987 he made around $125 million by selling it to more than 800 licensees in ninety-three countries. They sell merchandise worth more than $1 billion a year. Cardin's slice is from three to ten percent, yielding royalties of about $75 million, and it represents eighty-five percent of his turnover. Cardin is way ahead of the competition in numbers: Christian Dior has 300 licensees, Yves St Laurent 200, and Calvin Klein twelve.

When the modestly sized Swiss tobacco company F. J. Burrus made a bid for export sales in 1982, it opted for a licensing deal with Cardin, rather than spending the huge sums needed to create a new world brand. 'We needed a door opener,' Burrus told *Forbes* magazine. During 1987 the company sold ten million packs of 'Cardin' cigarettes, producing the man himself an income of $225,000 a year.

Other Cardin products range from clocks to deodorants. Even Cardin has lost track of exactly how many there are. Certainly his personal involvement with how they look ranges from the perfunctory to the non-existent. 'Even we don't know all the products we license,' Edouard Saint Bris, Cardin's director of licensing, was once incautious enough to admit to *The New York Times*.

But then it is not Cardin's expertise that is in demand, but his name. Two decades of frenetic licensing have ensured that though he has long fallen from grace as a star of the Paris collections, the income from his licensing activities has never been higher. His name may not cut the dash it once did on the catwalks, but when it comes to shifting mid-market cologne to the upwardly mobile, or commanding premium prices for Japanese-made biros, Cardin has just the right hint of status. The name sounds a little bit special, a little bit different, in middle America and provincial

61

Japan. What makes him so attractive for the aspirational classes is that though his products may sound expensive, they are actually affordable. How much longer his signature and trademark stay desirable, given the fact that now even the Soviet Union's Ministry of Light Industry is a licensee, remains open to doubt.

After twenty years Pierre Cardin cologne still generates revenues of $30 million worldwide, but in America at least there are worrying signs for him that the name is losing its magic. Cardin's staff make no bones about it, it is the licensees who are in the driving seat. 'The best way to stop people copying his designs is to have licensees who pay a minimum guarantee and a royalty, because if you can buy the original, a copy becomes less interesting. We send about 20,000 sketches a year all around the world. Monsieur Cardin has the original idea, and it is then adapted by our designers,' Saint Bris explains.

But now after a career spent using other people's money to make the products that bear his name, it is Cardin's own money that is behind the shaky-looking Maxim's licensing empire. Cardin bought up 100 percent control of the rights to exploit the venerable Maxim's name at the end of the 1970s. When Cardin opened up Maxim's restaurant in New York, it cost him $10 million of his own money, and lost $300,000 in its first year. That was despite preparing the ground with painstaking thoroughness. To add a little cultural sparkle to the Maxim's name, Cardin went to the length of erecting a replica of the original restaurant inside the Metropolitan Museum of Art in New York in 1982, ostensibly as part of the museum's La Belle Epoque exhibition, which he sponsored to the tune of $500,000. Cardin stood in the receiving line at the private view greeting the usual celebrities. Pat Buckley, Nancy Kissinger, Betsy Bloomingdale, Calvin Klein, Bill Blass all turned up, but celebrities have been conspicuous by their absence in the New York Maxim's since it officially opened

Lost in an endless forest of products that carry his signature, Pierre Cardin occasionally has time for a photo opportunity to prove that he hasn't forgotten how to sign his name

for business in 1985. The reviews were less than glowing, and the power lunchers stayed away in droves.

In London, Cardin was less financially exposed, but his partners Kennedy Brookes came badly unstuck. In the end they were forced to turn the reproduction Belle Epoque main dining room into a wine bar, and banished Maxim's into the attic.

When Cardin considered getting involved in the New York hotel business his accountants carried out a study concluding that guests would pay as much as $280 a night if the hotel was called Maxim's. Cardin cited this to back up his claims to a $500,000 fee from the hotel in its first year, simply for letting it use the Maxim's name. His partner was Jack Pratt, a Texan developer who started in fast food and Holiday Inns and wanted to move into the grand hotel league. He had thought about buying the Ritz name, but couldn't afford it, then talked to Yves St Laurent, Givenchy, and Gucci, but nothing came of it. Cardin settled on a $100,000 advance for every hotel Pratt opened with the Maxim's name and 1.5 percent of gross revenues. The consistent failure of Maxim's restaurant to become a major venue in a city where food is all about status, didn't do much for Cardin's bargaining position. The flop of Maxim's peanuts didn't help either, and excited sharp questions about whether grand hotels and peanuts naturally went together under the same name.

The devaluation of their names is not the only potential hazard for people who sell their celebrity for commercial ends. Back in 1986, when the A. J. Obie investment company went bust, an aggrieved customer from Chicago filed a suit against the company's star endorsers, including actor George Hamilton, for enticing them into a questionable enterprise. But the threat of legal proceedings when things go wrong has not, so far at least, done much to deter celebrities from lending their names to businesses of which they have little or no knowledge.

CHAPTER FOUR

THE FASHION SYSTEM

It's that white t-shirt again. James Dean had one and Giorgio Armani wears one all the time. Utterly serious about his image, Armani likes to show that he can relax too

Giorgio Armani is a busy man. He has ten collections to design. He has an international corporation that turned over $350 million in 1987 to run. There are the details of the contract he has just signed with the Japanese to open fifty shops from Tokyo to Osaka to ponder. But there is still time to talk about the essentials. He leans across the table in his office, a handsome eighteenth-century room large enough to stage grand opera in, and decorated with frescoes featuring Neptune brandishing his trident at suitably impressed water nymphs. Gilded classical columns flank the floor-to-ceiling windows that look out over the courtyard. There are mirrors everywhere, white flowers on the desk, and a carpet of what appears to be suede which induces a semi-religious hush.

Armani, looking fit, tanned, and absurdly youthful for a man in his fifties, despite his snow white hair, is in casual shirtsleeves. He looks a picture of the Italian idea of a clean-cut American. But you still feel like calling him sir, and standing up when he walks into a room. After all, this is a palace. In fact, the Caproni family, from whom Armani rents it, still live in one corner of their ancestral home. And the espresso comes on a silver tray, wafted in by a butler in a white apron and a uniform jacket. Armani is genial, but you sense a certain imperious will behind the good humour. 'Are you difficult to work with?' I enquire. He smiles: 'No . . . I do shout at people once in a while, and I did break an ashtray once, but no.'

There isn't much doubt about where Armani gets his outfits. His neat white shirt has a discreet label that bears his own name attached to the breast pocket. In his dressing room, the wall of wardrobes, protected by electrically operated up-and-over garage doors, is stacked high with Armani shirts, fresh off the production line, and still in their neat cellophane bags. The hanging space is full of well-ordered, disciplined ranks of suits, ties, underwear, bathrobes, shoes, gloves, jeans, coats, and scarves. All of them

67

have his name on them too. For that matter, so do the telephone, the cologne – advertised with posters that carry a carefully art-directed version of his signature – and the table lights.

Of course, these are not literally Armani products. It is not an Armani factory that makes them. It is not Armani money that is at stake in producing them. As far as the telephone with its fluorescent stripe that lights up to signify an incoming call, or the cologne in its light-bulb shaped bottle, or the shoes, and a lot of other things are concerned, Armani's involvement is limited to approval. He simply sells his signature, and the licensees, provided that they meet his standards, bask in reflected Armani glory. Sometimes there may be an Armani sketch, translated into detailed instructions by one of his assistants. But the point about an Armani product is not what it is, but who it is signed by.

Nor are the 'Armani' shops all that they seem. Many are not, in fact, Armani property. They belong instead to retailers who buy a franchise to use the name. The single-designer shop has become an essential part of the panoply of the new breed of fashion heroes. It's a more powerful and concentrated way of selling fashion than the traditional department stores, with their racks of clothes by different designers hanging side by side. It puts the focus on the name of the designer, and the image he is trying to put across.

What Armani has done is to create a name with an aura that is as desirable for manufacturers and retailers today as one of the old film stars was for the Hollywood studios. And like them he takes a percentage of the box office gross. Armani is the Midas of modern consumerism. Everything to which he puts his name – clothes, umbrellas, or suitcases – can command higher prices than exactly the same product without the right label. Even among Armani labels, an elaborate stratification system has been established. There is a world of difference between the Giorgio Armani white-on-black label, and the black-on-white version. And the distance between either of them and the brash GA eagle that signifies an Emporio Armani product is greater still. It is, in effect, a caste system, as precise as anything devised by the army, graded according to price, quality, and audience, and protected by teams of international lawyers who ensure that unauthorized manufacturers do not cash in without paying for the privilege. Ironically, the more desirable the Armani image becomes, the greater the attraction of pirating the name. Applying it to a cheap Portugese t-shirt, or a Taiwanese-made shopping bag, is to make a silk purse out of a sow's ear. The harder Armani works to maintain the value of his name, the more it is worth to the counterfeiters. The name 'Armani', applied even to a cheap garment that has nothing to do with the company, triggers a certain response from the most sophisticated consumers: one that is demonstrably different from that which comes from applying the words Cardin or Chanel to exactly the same garment. Obviously it's not simply the Armani personality itself that counts, but the way in which it is amplified and presented to a mass audience, almost as a performance.

In a sense, Armani's own policy of covering every sector of the market duplicates, rather more judiciously, the work of the counterfeiters who infest the fashion industry. It is a carefully measured strategy: clearly, selling to the mass market brings much higher rewards in the short term than selling a small number of high-priced items to the elite. But its appeal to an elite is what makes the Armani signature valuable. A lot of Armani's skill has been in the subtlety with which he has sliced the cake, appealing to consumers at every price level, without alienating any of them.

It's hard to believe that something as authoritative as the Armani brand has only been in existence since 1975. It manages to convey the impression of always having been there, as quintessentially Italian as La Scala or the Vespa. Yet the Armani style still feels relaxed and personal. This is Italy, after all, and Armani is a family business, just like Fiat; one where personalities and instincts count for as much as paper credentials. And even if the Armani label is just as rigorously promoted as IBM or Colonel Sanders, it doesn't seem as if it is. Or perhaps it is more accurate to say that its identity is not just skin deep. The aura created by the label is carefully reflected throughout the whole organization, even in the way its founder lives.

The Armani identity is based on a system of signs that are instantly recognizable to an initiate. What has happened is that the very name Armani has assumed a meaning that goes beyond taking the clothes themselves at face value. A jacket, after all, is just a jacket. But an Armani jacket is something rather different. It is a symbol of values that go beyond simple fashion. Wearing the Armani label is like driving a BMW: it's discreetly modern, subtly affluent, the mirror opposite of Ralph Lauren's nostalgia, for example. And it is partly this quality that has made Armani a modern Italian hero. It was the Americans who first made him famous and, for the Italians, keen to be taken seriously as a modern industrial power, not a simpatico but unreliable nation of hot-blooded Latins, that counted for a lot.

The Armani label is strong enough to be capable of meaning different things to different people. To the Saturday afternoon elite on the football terraces it's a badge of recognition, of having arrived, whether it's obtained in exchange for a shopping bag full of crumpled five-pound notes or by other, less respectable, means. But to a very different audience, made up of that curious breed of American businesswomen who insist on going to work in training shoes, carrying their high heels in a plastic bag to change into when they feel like delivering a carefully measured dose of sexuality, Armani has another, equally powerful meaning.

The astonishing thing is that Armani has, so far, managed to

Another Armani collection, this time for Brian De Palma's film _The Untouchables_

keep both audiences happy. Isn't he worried that opening a chain of Emporio Armani stores in Britain as he is planning will put his label within uncomfortably easy reach of the football hooligans who prize it as the ultimate status symbol? Won't that put off the gilded clientele of his Knightsbridge premises?

'People asked us the same thing in Italy when we launched the Armani Jeans range a few years ago, and of course it didn't happen. We keep making the quality and standards of the Giorgio Armani label higher and higher, and there is never any confusion between that and our other ranges.' Of course, even the rich want to feel that people can recognize the trappings of their wealth. Building up Armani's presence at the mass-market end, provided the top-of-the-line range keeps up the quality, doesn't hurt the recognition factor at all.

Initially it was the distinctive line of his clothes, his high-quality, Italian-made fabrics, and his mastery of tailoring that lifted Armani into orbit. Armani, like all the most successful fashion designers, has had the skill to produce the kind of clothes that flatter their wearers.

But now it's the skill with which he handles the image and identity of the brand, or, to put it another way, of his name, that counts just as much as the product he sells. The meaning of the Armani name is shaped by the look of the shops, with their subdued, flattering neutrality, the high-gloss finish of the shopping bags, the elegance of the typeface that he uses to spell out his signature, along with such ploys as getting his friend Martin Scorsese to direct a TV commercial for the company, and providing the clothes for De Palma's gore-soaked epic, _The Untouchables_, matching Ralph Lauren's involvement with _The Great Gatsby_. And the way that Armani himself lives and looks matters a lot – a fact of which he is only too well aware. Interestingly, Armani is shy of using his own picture to advertise the company,

71

unlike Ralph Lauren, who likes nothing better than being snapped lounging about in his kitchen in a snow white t-shirt, sipping beer from the bottle.

To interview Armani is to find a man of relaxed charm. But when his picture is being taken, he is considerably less relaxed. Magazines find themselves willy nilly agreeing to submit portraits of him for his approval. Words, after all, are secondary to pictures in the celebrity business, a fact with which such old hands at the game as Joseph Stalin were well acquainted. If Armani were fat, or ugly, it's unlikely that his business would have been the success that it has.

Armani has a healthy scepticism for the Mystery of The Label, but nevertheless treats his with the utmost respect. It is, after all, his most important asset. Every Armani garment comes with a card that looks like a banknote, guaranteeing its authenticity. In fact, given the grubby state of the average 1000-lire bill, it looks rather more valuable. Each card is stamped with a number, and printed with elaborate whirls and cross-hatches that have clearly tested the engraver's art to its limits.

Armani expects his customers to have minds of their own. 'I'm against people following fashion blindly. I hope people who wear my clothes use fashion to express themselves. They should be able to take parts of the collection and mix it with other things. The collection is designed for people to use with intelligence.'

But he has occasionally been disappointed by the reaction of his audience. At one point he thought about using detachable Velcro labels, and tried to make his name as unobtrusive as possible. It was not a successful move. 'The stores complained when their customers couldn't find the labels,' he says. 'It's not as simple as leaving the name on or off, people need to have something to identify with. They need to go beyond a signature, they need to know that there is something behind the myth.'

Outside one of his two offices in Milan, in the via Durini, a sombre yellow-ochre Milanese street that conceals internal splendour behind external austerity, is the world's first, and largest, branch of Emporio Armani. Most of the day you can see the sharply dressed teenagers who hang out on the street corner, pressing their noses to the plate glass. Few of them go in, intimidated perhaps by the air of calm inside. Immediately opposite is another shop, dedicated to children's clothes which carry the Armani label too. The window display there, full of impossibly cute outfits, looks as if it is aimed at parents who like dressing their infants up like Action Man dolls. Two doors along there is another shop, named Mani, which also turns out to sell Armani-designed clothes, this time for women, at mid-range prices. All of these are the real thing in Armani terms and yet, in another sense, none of them are. They feel like reverential temples of fashion, selling the stylish clothes that have made the master's name. And yet, they are not really what give Armani its glamour. The sanctum of sanctums is ten minutes away, in the via Borgonuovo, close to Armani's other office. Here there are no ifs and buts; the shop is simply called Giorgio Armani, and you can smell the money as soon as you pass through the photo-electrically operated doors. It's not money in the sense of gold bars and ostentatious jewellery, but in the costly look that comes from solid cashmere overcoats deep enough to drown in, and from a staff that seems as if it would be more at home trading financial futures on the New York stockmarket than selling socks. The low-profile price tags have enough noughts to sustain the illusion that you are in a bank.

Giorgio Armani was born in Piacenza in 1934. He dropped out of medical school after two years to start work as a buyer at Milan's La Rinascenta. He worked for a while as a designer for Cerrutti, and then set up on his own in 1975. It was Armani who practically invented power dressing for American women. He owes his instant popularity to an emerging generation of American yuppies, desperate to escape from their mannish Brooks Brothers office uniforms. Armani designed for the company, his friend and partner Sergio Galleotti took care of business. Turnover in the first year was £4 million, five years later that figure had gone up ten times, and it continued to grow rapidly. That growth did not falter, even after the tragically early death of Armani's partner in 1984, just at the point that the company was accelerating away to become a worldwide corporation with its own shops in America and Europe. Armani still feels the loss keenly. He took over responsibility for controlling company business, as well as design, and clearly in one sense his commitment to the continued growth of the company is a tribute to his friend.

You sense a certain emptiness in Armani's home. It is on top of the headquarters building, a glossy, clinical setting, in which every-thing, even each of the five baskets for his five Persian cats, is in exactly the right place. There is no clutter, no mess, and no art on the walls. His studio, two floors below, with its neat racks of fashion magazines, its shelves of magic markers, is the same: a study in neutrality. Only the giant-sized, five-foot high bottle of Armani scent behind his desk disturbs the studied calm. Visiting journalists get shown around by Armani's press assistant as part of the tour. The home is as much part of the business as the basement auditorium where catwalk shows introduce his autumn and spring collections to buyers and press, or the trademark itself.

The restrained colours, and austere setting, reflect Armani's approach to fashion perfectly. 'I design by taking the world, and filtering out all the things I don't like,' he says. In this context, the things that Armani doesn't like are noise, fuss, and brashness, or nostalgia.

Last year Armani told the Italian press that he was thinking about floating the company on the stock exchange, although quite why he would willingly relinquish control of a privately owned company to open it to the glare of financial scrutiny that public companies must expect, is hard to fathom. Certainly he has continued to grow with astonishing speed. Emporio Armani, which now accounts for almost half of the group's sales, has already passed the seventy stores mark, and plans are well advanced to make it more than one hundred by 1989, some wholly owned, others franchised.

'I want kids to be able to buy my clothes at Emporio, it will be the first step on the way to the main store for them.' It is also Armani's first step in reshaping the world in his own image. Armani is the model successful fashion hero. He looks the part, he lives the life. He has created a strongly identifiable image for his clothes, yet one with enough appeal to make it work across the whole market.

To succeed now, all fashion designers need to do the same. A designer like Azzedine Alaïa, for example, will never emerge beyond his dedicated but tiny audience while his range remains as limited as it is. Alaïa's clothes are all the same – blatantly sexual body wrapping. Similarly, Margaret Howell was stuck in a groove repeating her initially very successful lines based on re-creating handcrafted English reach-me-downs. There simply wasn't enough variety in her work to withstand the constant appetite of the media and the market for more and more novelty.

Paul Smith, on the other hand, stands a very good chance of achieving a status that will one day match that of Armani. He has the personality and the identity, as well as the breadth of approach, to take him onto a much larger stage. Already the Japanese have cottoned onto the value of Smith's name. There is a small chain of Paul Smith shops there and one of the giant fashion groups has turned out a carbon copy of the Smith look, inventing a fictitious character called Karl Helmut, whose trademark signature, used in all its shops in Japan, is all but indistinguishable from Smith's original.

The glamour and power of fashion was originally based on the theatrical attractions of the catwalks, on the charisma of the celebrities who wear the couture clothes which in fact form only an economically negligible fraction of the turnover of the big fashion names. The biannual collections provide a focus, reported in the newspapers and magazines. They create an impresssion of excitement and activity, turning fashion into a performance with an audience and its stars, just like sport or film. It is this impression that makes the investment involved – a minimum of £250,000, ranging up to £500,000 for a Paris show – worthwhile.

After the couture shows come the ready-to-wear shops themselves, calculatingly designed to convey an appropriate message and to be easily reproduced, stripped down to their fundamentals, in the shopping malls and the department stores. There is more at stake here than simple shop fitting. That's why Diane von Furstenburg in New York used Michael Graves, Esprit retained Ettore Sottsass, Norman Foster and Shiro Kuramata, and Katharine Hamnett commissioned Nigel Coates. The big costly shops set the tone, and define the approach. But the briskest business is often done in the smaller outlets within department stores, shops in shops, as they are called, where the essence of a fashion name may have to be put across in just a few square feet. It may be defined simply by a chair and a logo. Then there is the advertising used to create the aura around the designer's name.

But it is pre-eminently the power of the Paris collections to command attention that gives fashion names the glamour that makes them attractive to manufacturers outside the clothing business. Perfume, for example – the product, perhaps, most in need of the injection of a personality – has relied on using fashion names since the days of Dior and Chanel. Now it is Armani, Lauren, and the others who make the running. But only in the most abstract sense can perfume be said to embody the personality of the individual who lends it their name. Launching a new scent costs well over £5 million in Europe; in America it can be twice that figure. The licence revenue generated by perfume deals is therefore vital. In the early days of a designer's career, launching perfumes and accessories underscores their status.

Nobody is more tuned to the importance of a name, and creating the aura to go with it, than Ralph Lauren (*né* Lifshitz). The success of Lauren's $1000 million empire has been built up to a quite remarkable degree on the power of suggestion. Lauren made a fortune introducing the world to the kipper tie in the years after he first registered the Polo trademark in 1967. Since then one of his most important weapons has been an advertising campaign using photographer Bruce Weber, which has created a mythical and surprisingly complete world around the Lauren name. Shot initially in black and white – though now moving into colour, to distance itself from the increasing number of copycat monochrome campaigns – it centres on a regular cast of models who reappear month after month. They live in a curiously timeless world made up of images pieced deftly together out of a past that is not exactly the 1930s, nor the 1950s. 'Cary Grant, Fred Astaire, Duke of Windsor' says Lauren when asked about his influences. It's an admiration that has not, in all cases, been reciprocated. When Lauren called one of his jackets the Astaire, the grand old man asked him to stop, a request that was duly granted.

Curiously, Weber is also responsible for creating the equally lavish and radically different photographic image of Calvin Klein. Where Lauren dwells in a manufactured past, Klein's world as depicted by Weber is a muscle-beach wet dream. Klein's scent Obsession is depicted at the centre of a writhing sea of bodies. His

Ralph Lauren relaxes at home on the range. He has a white t-shirt too. Bruce Weber, who took this picture, works on both Lauren's and Calvin Klein's advertising campaigns

underpants are modelled by Olympian youths who look like something out of a Brownshirt fantasy. 'In this business,' Klein once remarked, 'everything we do is about creating an image.' That's what makes Weber one of the highest-paid photographers in the world, and it's what persuades Ralph Lauren to spend over $3 million a year on photography alone.

Lauren's clothes are not so much designed as researched, deliberately patterned on costumes from black and white films, and from the pages of old magazines. Lauren tries to make his clothes look as if they have not been bought from a shop, but simply acquired as part of the natural process of leisured upper-middle-class life, just as prep school boys are kitted out by traditional outfitters, and sons are measured for their bespoke suits by their father's tailors. They aren't meant to make you look fashionable, they are meant to establish your credentials.

Weber's photographs for Lauren depict picnics in the Hamptons, tennis parties, and scented, gracious homes. Parents in cashmere jackets and linen slacks shepherd children in wet bathing suits and towels. The cast of characters, some chosen for their lived-in faces, others, of both sexes, for their well-scrubbed virginal East Coast beauty, are seen slipping in and out of glossy black limousines from the 1940s, boarding liners, and at candlelit dinners in their dinner jackets. They are photographed in elegant rooms full of crocodile skin, mahogany, and flowers. The men wear braces and inhabit rooms full of old books, and, incongruously, well-oiled cricket bats.

These are images which can be expected to exert their greatest appeal among people who do not have such family backgrounds. This is not Lauren/Lifshitz's world – he was brought up in Mosholu Parkway in the Bronx – though he clearly wishes it was. He turns the past into the raw material for an unlimited dressing-up box, to play at being one of his childhood heroes. It's a cavalier attitude that has provoked an indignant protest from conservationists on at least one occasion. Back in 1982, his critics claimed that Lauren took his enthusiasm for American antique quilts to the extent of chopping up hundreds to provide raw material to decorate his own collection.

Even the launch of his denim ranges is presented in the wishful Lauren way. A big-boned, slab-faced model, his neatly kept hair combed back from his forehead – he could be a track athlete from the American team for the 1936 Olympics – is driving his open-topped Morgan. Over his shoulder is his dog. He wears a period watch and a school tie, along with a prefaded denim jacket, a silk handkerchief in the denim shirt pocket, and denim jeans. It is playing spare parts surgery with the past: denim was completely out of the question before the end of World War Two for anybody but poor Southerners – and they weren't exactly thrilled about wearing it either. Yet here it is, presented as being as much a part of a traditional gentleman's wardrobe as silver cufflinks.

The images duplicate, detail for detail, the now oddly innocent, even corny, preoccupations of advertising from the past. Treated with today's production values they exert a curious power. The copy for the Lauren denim advertisement, much more garrulous than is usual, tells the whole story. 'Crafted in the era when quality and durability were more important than fashion, they are constructed as an authentic expression of classic American work clothes.' Of course, the cost of Lauren's version of authenticity is anything up to 100 percent more than the originals on which it is modelled. And the tenses are curiously ambiguous, implying that these brand new garments are antiques.

With his dude ranch high up in the Rockies, Lifshitz self-consciously lives up to the Lauren message. Looking at old photographs of Lauren, you can take an archeological trawl through the strata on which the present version of the Lauren image has been built. The paleolithic age dates back to 1974 when Lauren first started appearing in ads boosting his products. In those days he wore three-piece suits, looking like a sawn-off Tom Jones, the tulip-shaped lapels of his jacket protruding way beyond his shoulders and set off by a high-rise collar. After that came the right stuff: faded denim, soft leather pilot's jackets, oddly out of synch with the would-be aristo image his ads project today.

The ads are placed in long runs in the magazines, a dozen pages at a time, more potent, and certainly far more costly to produce, than the editorial pages around them. To put them together, Lauren enlists the help of seasoned fashion journalists: Ann Boyd, once the fashion editor of *The Sunday Times*, played an important part in shaping the image. The product is all but invisible in the advertising photographs: three Jack Russell terriers sit on an ancient foot stool, a man in his fifties with a face that shows the effect of the passing years, his moustache full and silver, gazes through floor-length windows. This is meant to look real. A parquet floor that has seen generations of housemaids polish it with beeswax, casts a mellow glow. A bedside table carries a cascade of silver-framed photographs, all black and white; there are cut-glass clocks, silver boxes, and Biedermeier furniture.

The message is unambiguous: the scent of old money, fashion for those who don't want to look fashionable but who do want to look secure. To bring the image to life Lauren has constructed a temple dedicated to the Lauren way of life: the old Rhinelander Mansion on Madison Avenue has been turned at enormous cost into a temple of new old money, and would-be WASP style. Fourteen million dollars were poured into creating what is a half-English-country-house, half-Hollywood version of a South Kensington department store. It carefully blurs the lines between merchandise and decoration, between antique and new, between original and reproduction. There are piles of battered leather hat-boxes, re-creations of a prep school attic and a Wiltshire gun room.

The only discordant note is the presence of the Lauren security force, neat but muscular men bulging out of their preppie blazers, muttering into their walkie-talkies. Perhaps they should be kitted out as cowboys to bring the other Lauren dream to life. Here you can see scrawny New York ladies living the fantasy: they come in shopping for an outfit, and as they sit in the little parlour upstairs they really believe that they are Wallis Simpson, in for a fitting.

The patina of age is vital to the illusion: not just in the piles of junk, hoovered up from the tatty end of the Fulham Road and shipped out by the container load, but even in the newly manufactured clothes. The sportswear department, for instance, is full of artificially aged garments, prewashed, prefaded, prefabricated.

Lauren could sell tickets for his private museum. And he has not been shy of using real museums to underscore the authority of his name in exactly the same way. It was Lauren who sponsored Diana Vreeland's Man and the Horse show at the New York Metropolitan Museum a few years ago. Lauren's Polo trademark appeared in the museum itself and the exhibition looked like a gigantic advertisement for the Lauren look. The whole point is to bring to flesh the images created by Weber's photography.

The result of all this is to create an aura of quality around the Lauren trademark. The image becomes so strong that it eclipses and overtakes the actual products. So much so that when you buy a pair of socks, or a Lauren towel, from a Bloomingdales Lauren department in a mall in suburban New York, you still feel that you are taking a sliver of that original Lauren style away with you. In Britain, beer is sold in exactly the same way. Advertising creates a personality for the various identical-tasting brews. 'The punters drink the ads,' as one creative director in London puts it.

It is a process that, by no means incidentally, has the effect of adding value to merchandise. At its most extreme, the kind of arithmetic involved is demonstrated by the discovery of Mabel Foxwell in 1982 by *The Sunday Times*. She was an outworker knitting pullovers to sell to Lauren at £6 each. These, under the gloss of the Lauren label, promptly commanded £170 at the Bond Street store, and £245 in New York. But then Lauren is spending $17 million a year on advertising.

There are short cuts to creating the persona that Lauren has built up over the years. When the Hong Kong manufacturer Murjani looked for a way into the American market for jeans ten years ago, it signed up Warren Hirsch as its New York manager to help persuade a sceptical American public. His strategy was crude, but, in the short term at least, effective. Hirsch decided that the way to sell an unknown third-world product was to identify it with something that would attract the imagination of the Americans and persuade them that they were getting something highly desirable. In essence it was the art of persuading people to buy a product for $40 that they wouldn't buy at $10. 'What we were looking for was not just a designer, but a name that stood for American royalty,' remembers Hirsch. 'We had about twenty names on our original list including Lee Radziwill and Charlotte Ford. Gloria Vanderbilt was my second choice after Jackie Onassis.' Apparently it was Vanderbilt's 'artistic' talent, as well as her name, that tipped the scales in her favour – she had dabbled in linen, spice jars, and greetings cards before agreeing to do the Murjani job – after Onassis turned them down.

Gloria Vanderbilt was the original poor little rich girl. Her great-great-grandfather was the railway king, Commodore Cornelius Vanderbilt. Her aunt had introduced the Prince of Wales to Wallis Simpson, underlining an aspect of the Duke of Windsor legend that Ralph Lauren would be unlikely to want to focus on. But despite the robber baron family heritage, it was Murjani's

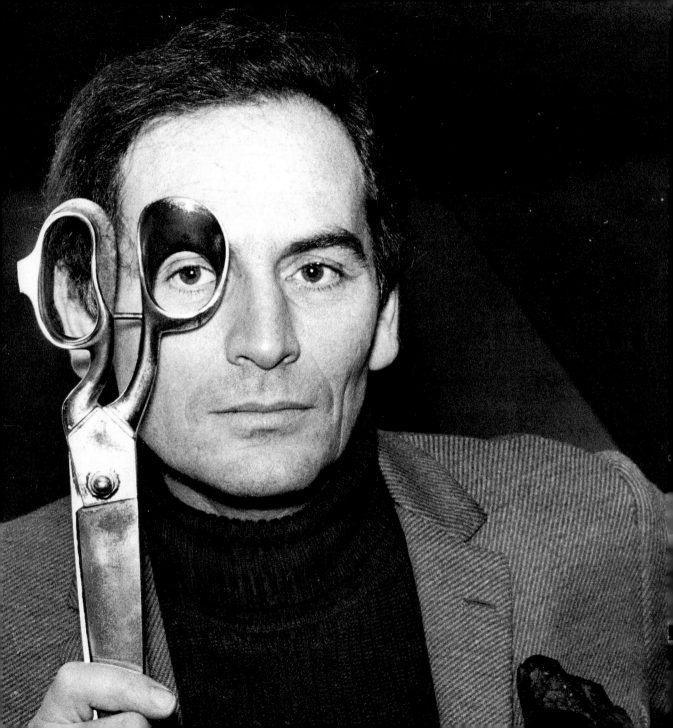

Perhaps the only thing Cardin didn't license from his early days as a couture star were his scissors

success at selling the jeans that bore her name which made Gloria rich. She signed a contract for what the company described as 'the high seven figures', to lend her name and image to jeans for Murjani. It specified, among other things, ninety days of personal appearances a year. She brought, in addition to her name stitched across the back pocket of hundreds of millions of pairs, her swan logo: 'From my favourite role in my favourite play, Molnar's *The Swan*,' she explained.

Despite her disconcertingly old world habit of calling jeans 'slacks', Vanderbilt did the company proud, extolling the virtues of jeans cut to fit the female shape. 'You don't have to lie on the floor to zip up my slacks, yet they are constructed so that they don't gape at the back.' In her first year for Murjani, sales went up sixfold, and would eventually reach $750 million. TV commercials were considered a vital part of the picture, which put Vanderbilt to work again. Ten percent of revenues were ploughed back into commercials. In 1978–80 these cost $10 million. 'They really hug your derr-ee-ere, Vanderbilt jeans hit all the best places,' went the incessant jingle.

And in 1980, when Vanderbilt launched the range in Britain, she naturally chose the House of Lords for the party. 'Our bottoms are tops,' she claimed. However, Vanderbilt jeans, despite attempts to diversify into other areas, was essentially a one-product company. Further, the company lacked the retail outlets that could be used to project the image more strongly. It was a lesson quickly learned by Lauren, Armani, and others, who quickly shifted into retailing themselves. The market soon became saturated with competition, and when the idea of designer jeans faded, Vanderbilt faded with it. Murjani had already bought the rights to her name. Company strategy had abused and over-used Vanderbilt's signature. It was handled only in the interest of the short-term maximum extraction of profit. Vanderbilt went on to license handbags, scent, and, unbelievably, tofu. Meanwhile Murjani has moved on to the Coca-Cola clothing range: a name no less venerable than Vanderbilt's, and, conveniently, one already the subject of saturation TV advertising to whose coat-tails they could hang.

It is a direction in which Pierre Cardin, the king of the licensing business, to whom both Armani and Lauren owe a considerable debt in terms of business approach if not creative input, seems to be moving too.

Cardin is a man who created himself. Born, according to some accounts, Piero Cardini, in the countryside north of Venice, he moved to Paris in the years after the Second World War. He worked for Dior, then started his own fashion house. Cardin is the man who established the fashion designer as hero on a sound business footing. And when he signed up his first licensee, for Cardin ties in 1956, he was starting something big. In those days the Cardin name stood for the hard edge of modernism. It was as chic and French as a Citroen DS19. Cardin presented himself as a revolutionary. His clothes made a lot out of strong colour, unorthodox geometry, and flashy materials. Unlike Lauren, Cardin, while he was still a creative designer, produced fantasies about technology and the future, rather than tradition and the past. He was seen escorting Jeanne Moreau around the world. Simca asked him to design a car for them. But all that is long gone now. Cardin lives on the residue of having been fashionable. His models – and his designs – seem to sleepwalk down the runway.

Cardin established his place in history by talking himself into it. He paints a semi-mystical picture of getting his first job in fashion, being directed to meet his first employer by a passer-by. 'I was Dior's first employee,' he also claims regularly, with more enthusiasm than veracity. Cardin has just managed to stay inside the rules set by the Chambre Syndicale. To qualify as a couturier he must make custom-tailored clothes, employ twenty-three seamstresses, and present at least two collections of at least seventy-five models a year. He exudes boundless self-confidence. 'Couture still gives me the most pleasure, and it is the reason my name is so strong. I need the prestige of my name as a couturier to publicize my other interests. I lose a great deal of money on couture, a very great deal. I have been in the sky for thirty-three years, and nobody else in Paris has been on the front page of creativity for so long. Chanel is always the same story, the same suit. Dior is nice, but not creative. Only Pierre Cardin remains.'

The Cardin path is still, in essence, the one that the new fashion names all tread, even such an iconoclast as Christian Lacroix, who is busy creating an empire with all the usual trappings. Lacroix is a third generation would-be fashion hero. A former employee of Hermès, and Patou, he has been deliberately groomed for international stardom, a self-conscious creation based on the experience of his predecessors. He was launched with a £5 million investment by Financière Agache, the company behind the house of Dior. With the Lacroix mansion in the Faubourg St Honoré, the spectacular couture shows of attention-grabbing if all-but-unwearable clothes, the Lacroix phenomenon amounts to an attempt to create a multinational as much as a fashion house. The investment is high, but then the potential rewards are enormous. If Lacroix turns out to be the next Armani, then it will have been repaid scores of times over. And clearly that is his ambition. By the time the Lacroix couture collection was launched in the autumn of 1987, catapulting him from obscurity with his photogenic clothes, the ready-to-wear line, aimed where the real money is, was already being mapped out. The Lacroix timetable is to put accessories in the shops at around the same time, with perfume and menswear scheduled for 1989.

CHAPTER FIVE

DESIGNER CELEBRITY

Michael Graves took architecture out of the ghetto and into the brand name era. But Graves himself runs the risk of becoming better known for his kettles – even Nancy Reagan has one – than his buildings

Charles Jencks, self-styled pope of post-Modernism, has made a lot of mileage claiming that the biggest thing to happen to design in the last fifty years has been the death of modern architecture. Gleefully he dated its demise to 1973, the precise moment of the dynamiting of the notorious Pruitt Igoe flats in St Louis, the award-winning, architect-admired but resident-hated, high-rise development that was planned as a utopia, but turned into a slum before it was finished.

Now, much to Jencks's distress, Pruitt Igoe has been supplanted as an architectural landmark by *Women's Wear Daily*, the fashion paper that loves by turns to fawn over and then sink its glossy talons into the reputations of the rich and famous. The day in 1984 that *W*, as it snappily calls its weekly offshoot, printed a portrait of the diminutive architect Michael Graves will, in the long run, prove to be a more significant event than the premature demise of yet another troublesome teenage building.

There was Graves, jostling for position on the page with the likes of Gloria von Thurn und Taxis, Klaus von Bülow and Stephanie of Monaco, with his gleaming, even smile and macho aviator spectacles – desk-bound architects can look tough too – partially obliterated by a red cross and scarred by the word 'out'.

'I've been out so long, it seems like in to me,' Graves told *Vanity Fair* at the time. It was positive proof that architecture and design had become part of the fashion system, subject to the same fluctuations of rapidly acquired popularity, and even more rapid falls from favour. The more photogenic architects and designers had finally gained the kind of celebrity value enjoyed by successful tennis players and film stars. Given the fact that less than five years previously *W*'s readers would have been hard put to tell you who Frank Lloyd Wright was, let alone put a name to any living architect, it was a remarkable development.

Architecture had emerged from dusty obscurity and become a

subject that was being talked about – not with any great consequence perhaps, but at least being discussed – at smart dinner parties. Gradually the -isms of private architectural debate invaded the conversation of professional taste makers. And such conventional architectural trappings as Le Corbusier chaise longues, maple strip floors, and curious artefacts involving halogen began to crop up as fashionable props outside the architectural bunker.

Architects, blinking mole-like in the sudden glare of unfamiliar exposure, were nonplussed at first. They had become so used to the pain of public indifference to their very existence, punctuated by the occasional high-rise witch hunt, that they could not understand why anyone would be interested in them.

But after Philip Johnson had managed to get onto the cover of both the London and New York *Times*, as well as *Time* magazine, with his design for the AT&T's Chippendale-topped skyscraper, before so much as a brick had been laid in anger, architecture suddenly became a high-profile subject. And for architects, publicity quickly turned from an unfamiliar novelty into an addiction.

The money-flaunting corporations of the 1980s, in a hurry to make their mark, found that hiring the right architect could be a useful short cut. It bestowed cultural credibility, got you noticed as a patron of the arts, qualified for tax breaks, and needn't cost that much more than putting up a standard developer's box.

Hotels had learned the same lesson in the 1970s: John Portman's mirror-glass monsters attracted the kind of press coverage that advertising money could never buy, all for the price of hiring the right architect. His Bonaventura hotel in Los Angeles became a symbol for the city, just as the Peachtree did for Atlanta.

What these architects designed – provided that it got into print or film – was less important than who they were. So when Michael Graves was hired by the Humana Corporation to design them a skyscraper in the provincial backwaters of Louisville, the point was less to provide a headquarters, more to build a monument to private medicine in general, and Humana in particular.

In fact, the Humana tower, just like AT&T, is, after all is said, a humdrum office building behind its gaudy skin, with the usual mundane acres of repetitive open-plan offices. What really attracted attention around the world was the architectural signature attached to it. Of course, to describe a building as its architect's creation, is misleading too. It hardly needs saying that one individual does not create a building. Major structures are planned by dozens of people, and built by hundreds, often using off-the-shelf components that their designer has never seen. But the *image* of what the architect does casts him in the role of the solitary genius, and it is that, myth or not, which makes the architect a star.

The fact that Graves was already notorious for putting up buildings which got noticed, was certainly no handicap to that strategy. And *W*'s strictures didn't do him any financial damage either. Graves looks just as likely to go down in history as the first Princeton professor to do shoe commercials, and to pick up $75,000 in royalties for designing a kettle, as for his architecture. But given a climate in which architecture is now an essential ingredient of the soaps – think about the mirror-glass towers that form a backdrop for the Dallas credits, and the hot pastels of Architectonica condominiums that announce Miami Vice – perhaps Graves is on the right historical track.

The Hong Kong and Shanghai Bank had much the same idea as Humana when they commissioned Norman Foster to build their new headquarters. They chose an architect with a well-known name as part of a deliberate policy to present themselves to the world as an organization of international standing and prestige.

Ten years before, to be seen spending money on architecture

was considered an unthinkable extravagance bordering on the certifiable. Concrete shoe-boxes, even expensive concrete shoe-boxes, might be dull, but they were at least reckoned to be respectable enough not to frighten the shareholders. By the end of the 1970s things had changed enough for the Hong Kong and Shanghai Bank to decide to spend £650 million on its Foster skyscraper, and to put its picture on their banknotes.

In the herbivorous days a decade ago, an architect like Foster, piloting himself around the world in a private jet, keeping a string of helicopters, would have been equally unthinkable. Once the architectural world was divided into two camps: the big firms, whose partners dressed in sharp pinstripes and did the commercial work without any pretensions that what they were doing had any wider cultural significance; and the academically respectable architects who had hair over their collars, wore suede shoes, designed private houses, the occasional art gallery, and kept to their ivory towers. Now the lure of the architectural big time has allowed the latter camp to crowd out the old-time hacks. The herbivores have had their revenge at last, picked up their mobile telephones, sharpened their 6B pencils, and trampled the carnivores. Needless to say, the results have been less than impressive. In architectural terms, the building boom of the 1980s has simply demonstrated that, given enough rope, the herbivores are just as capable of putting up monstrous monoliths as the commercial hacks.

The commercial discovery of architecture has eerie echoes of the way in which the pioneers of the Modern movement presented themselves in the 1920s and 30s. Le Corbusier, Mies, and Wright were themselves all consummate image manipulators. Staring fixedly at the camera in contemporary portraits, they self-consciously adopted the poses of recruiting posters, gazing out over the heads of their humble contemporaries into a bright but far-off future. They were bent on redesigning the world, so not surprisingly they reinvented themselves: pipes, bow ties, flowing cloaks, Euclidian spectacles, all became trademarks.

Their manifestos, and insistence on abstracting architecture through photography, combined to divorce them from reality. Their buildings were presented free of the constraints of daily life, subtly reinforcing the message that what they were doing was an act of pure artistic creation. What has changed mainly is that the audience for their successors has grown immeasurably. The pioneers were part of a tiny elite. Today's fashionable architects end up working for Disneyland, and turn up in the pages of *People*.

Attracting attention has become more and more difficult since then. Johnson's AT&T tower in New York, with its rose-granite walls and its baronial sky lobbies, got up to look like something out of a Douglas Fairbanks Jnr movie at his most swashbuckling, had things easy. Surrounded by graph-paper boxes, it couldn't help but make its presence felt. And it had Mayor Koch, clearly not a man given to understatement, gushing about a modern 'masterpiece'. But as the skylines of the world's skyscraper cities have been transformed by a wave of conspicuous newcomers which, in their attempts to out-do each other, make the 1960s look like the good old days, the stakes have been raised. Buildings like Humana become ever more whimsical and arbitrary. They quickly come to function as giant billboards, as they struggle to make themselves heard against the din of the competition.

In Pittsburgh, the local glass manufacturer commissioned Johnson to produce them a fifty-storey two-dimensional version of the Houses of Parliament, clad in one of their products. In Houston, the Republic Bank built another of Johnson's foibles, a sixty-storey version of the Dutch gable style. They are buildings that have little to do with architecture, or their context, everything to do with architect celebrities and their signature. Corporations use their work in just the same way that some people use Louis Vuitton luggage.

As architects became public property, their influence began to spill into other areas beyond simple building. Skyscrapers began to pop up in advertising campaigns, allowing a wide range of products, from Rothman's cigarettes to Wrigley's chewing gum, to bask in reflected architectural glory.

Perfume manufacturers talk about styling their bottles to 'look architectural'. Ira Levy, a New York designer for Estée Lauder, deliberately modelled the Aramis 900 bottle on Johnson's AT&T building; not, perhaps, the most flattering of comparisons for the latter, but one which the company believed would add to the appeal of its products with the upwardly mobile. Of course, the two reinforce each other. One modern building can look much the same as another, despite the fond hopes of its creators, until, that is, they start popping up on billboards. Then, when the buildings become famous thanks to the exposure they get in advertising, they in turn reinforce the product's image. Commercials simply end up selling buildings, and underline the metamorphosis of architects into celebrities.

The new breed of developers love buildings that get noticed. Putting up conspicuous buildings makes them into celebrities too. Donald Trump, currently the most notorious of the species, goes so far as naming his New York developments after himself, modestly bracketing himself with the Medicis and the Rockefellers. Trump Tower, with its sullen mirror glass irresistibly suggesting a cosmetics counter in a down-market department store, now dominates Fifth Avenue. It was followed by plans for Trump Plaza, Trump Castle, and the Trump Taj Mahal.

Trump personifies name brand developing. He is the man who used to fit out the doormen at the Trump Tower in guardsmens' scarlet tunics and bearskins in summer, and cossack uniforms in

Donald Trump, the developer with the towering ego, hired Philip Johnson – the architect who put the AT & T building on the cover of *Time* magazine – to design Trump Castle, but he never got around to building it

winter. Now that Trump is going for the understated look, they are got up like footmen from Claridge's. Trump, highly selectively, displays architectural critics' reviews in the lobby of the Trump Tower like theatre notices. Along with a band of other equally flamboyant figures, Trump has done his best to turn development from being a cool, calculating business, run by faceless men in back offices, into a headline-grabbing circus. Thanks to such attention-provoking stunts as rescuing a country widow from eviction by the banks, then inviting her up to New York for the typically understated gesture of the public burning of her mortgage in the Trump Tower atrium, Trump has made himself unquestionably the most famous developer in America. However, he is still only the twenty-seventh largest. In the face of his relentless quest for publicity, the fact that in New York itself Trump has only built three relatively modest structures, tends to disappear behind the smoke and mirrors.

In New York the towering egos of Trump and his competitors have battled it out in a juvenile playground struggle to build the tallest apartment tower in the city, and then the tallest building in the world. Would-be rival Harry Macklow, owner of the soaring black-glass Metropolitan Tower that looms over the Russian Tea Rooms, keeps a chart showing the comparative height of all the city's condo towers in his office, and uses specially commissioned movies to sell the apartments in his developments.

Trump is so desperate to win that he went as far as rewriting history on the lift control panels of the Trump Tower. The city stopped him going to the full seventy storeys he had in mind, so Trump righted this slight by adjusting the numbering on the lift buttons. As far as Trump is concerned, even bad publicity is better than no publicity. When *New York* magazine covered Trump's legal tribulations with some of his tenants in a less than

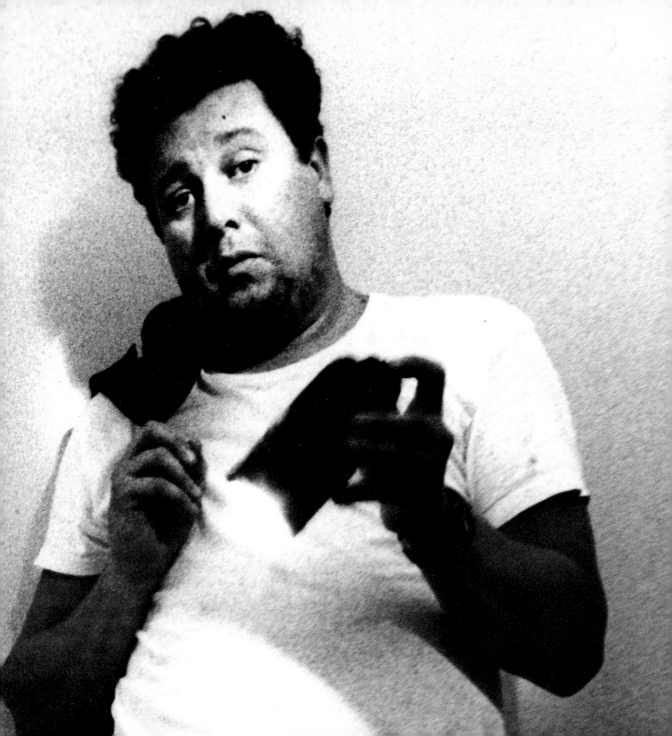

flattering light, he was all set to cancel his advertising – until he discovered that he was on the cover.

Trump takes himself seriously enough to have published – written is something of an exaggeration – a book to get his message across. He buys space in *The New York Times* to publicize his idiosyncratic views on the foreign policy of the United States. But apotheosis has finally come: Cadillac has licensed the Trump name for its top-of-the-line stretched limos. They will be delivered complete with on-board fax machines, telephones, and shredders, and with the Trump name emblazoned on the back so that nobody will miss the point.

The impact of celebrity on architecture does not stop with the developers. The fashionable world is more interested in shopping and lunching than sitting in offices. The idea of signing up a top-name architect to design your shop or restaurant was one that occurred to people quickly. It was in any case a chance to get a little creative synergy going. So a profession that less than a decade ago was still burdened down by the weight of its self-appointed historic mission of building a utopian world of eternally sunlit new towns, was soon busy producing exquisitely crafted little shops, bars, and restaurants. From there it was the shortest of steps for people who had spent six years slogging away at college, equipping themselves with the cultural and scientific equipment to remodel whole cities, to turn instead to such earthshaking cultural projects as designing shopping bags for Bloomingdales, decorating dinner plates, and designing cuckoo clocks. As an endeavour, it echoes the eagerness of advertising agencies to hire film directors like Francis Ford Coppola and Ken Russell to direct their TV commercials. The historical comparison would be asking Mozart to compose jingles. But, of course, that has happened retrospectively, without his consent, with the result that his music is diminished by endless

repetition as part of the sales pitch for motorcars, carpets, and cigars.

Designers, a previously unknown species, have long been poor relations to the architects. They used to be called commercial artists, auxiliaries for the printing industry, but now they too have become stars, partly on the strength of the success of their architectural colleagues.

To take the most cynical of viewpoints, it is possible to define design as anything that sells more product. And if you put on one side all his rhetoric about art and culture, then that is exactly what Raymond Loewy, the man who more than anyone turned design into a commercial business, was doing when he redesigned the Gestetner company's duplicator in 1924. He transformed what was an apparently arbitrary collection of wheels, cogs, wires, and handles, that looked a lot like the inside of a washing machine, and turned it into an essential item of modern office equipment simply by making the casing look different.

In his day, Loewy always ran the risk of being written off as nothing more than a showman. The more puritanical of design historians never took him seriously. But in the long term his influence has been enormous. Perhaps Loewy's most important contribution to the way that design is now practised was his very early realization of the opportunities that the celebrity system could bring a designer, especially at a time when it was an occupation that was hardly taken seriously. Loewy hired a publicity consultant with the specific task of getting him on to the cover of *Time* magazine – clearly an organ that has had a lasting impact on designers over the years. To this end he was forever being photographed, immaculate in dapper suit and martial moustache, striking dramatic poses with large pieces of streamlined machinery. He even went so far as to have a highly idealized version of his office constructed in New York's Museum of Modern Art.

Loewy practically designed himself, to become the personification of the designer as celebrity. Never one to miss out on claiming a slice of the credit where credit was not necessarily due, Loewy was quickly implying that he had designed just about everything that passed through his hands, from the Coca-Cola bottle to NASA spacecraft. Loewy succeeded in his assault on *Time* magazine, and became, in the American mind at least, the popular personification of what design was. With his unshakeable ego, and his unblushing conviction of his own worth, he created a model for the modern design superstar.

Raymond Loewy was one of the first to realize that products as seen by the consumer had personalities and identities. And in the last resort, the personality of the product is the personality of the designer. That was the point of Loewy having himself photographed lording it over the Studebaker Avanti, the car he claimed to have designed singlehanded.

Since it is all but impossible to create a cult of personality around an anonymous team of technicians and engineers, the Loewy portraits helped to create the myth of the omnipotent designer. And it is a myth that has gone on growing in power. Hence the Mazda car company's decision twenty-five years later to introduce its Alain Delon saloon. All that differentiates it from hundreds of thousands of other cars that come rolling off the Mazda production lines each year are the initials AD painted on to the doors, the ignition key equipped with the same initials, and the lurid seat upholstery. What Mazda is trying to sell is a fantasy, to inject its cars with the arrogant, dangerous charm of Delon himself. Detroit tried a variation on the same line: clearly a country with a speed limit of a sedate 55mph is not in a position to put Delon's mercurial personality on the roads. Instead Cadillac came up with specials, by, among others, fashion designers Bill Blass and Halston.

With the Italian Mario Bellini slightly different factors are at work. Bellini, again through the medium of a large office full of professionals, does have a more direct impact on how products actually look than any of the film stars and fashion designers who put their names on cars, although by no means in the Michelangeloesque manner that the elevation of his name implies. Bellini's signature, injection moulded across the back of a cassette player, is there to imply none too convincingly that this is a descendant of a hand-crafted Stradivarius.

The French designer Philippe Starck plays much the same game. His career was launched with the kind of boost that is a gift to a natural self-publicist. He was commissioned by Francois Mitterand to design the president's private office at the Elysée Palace.

Starck presents himself as an innocent and, at first sight, cuts an unlikely figure as an international design superstar. In contrast to the melancholy grace of Ettore Sottsass, or the well-cut elegance of Vico Magistretti, Starck regularly sports a black t-shirt that has clearly been slept in. He is paunchy, with facial stubble well beyond the limits of what could conceivably be called 'designer', and wears a denim jacket, beret, and Harley Davidson biker's scarf.

It doesn't seem to put off the Neiman Marcuses and the Dallas night-club owners who clamour to sign him up that Starck breaches the dress codes of the expense account restaurants that they take him to, or that he will bring out his own clasp knife to tackle his steak with. Nor does Starck's Leftism – these days confined mainly to pedalling around New York on his bicycle, rather than travelling by limo – bother people. The Starck signature is bankable – something which recommended him to Steve Rubell, notorious former owner of Studio 54, who is currently engaged on building a new fortune by opening up terminally fashion-conscious hotels in Manhattan. Rubell's formula is breathtakingly simple: he buys run-down old flop houses with tiny rooms and cockroaches in the kitchen. He guts them, has them redesigned by designer celebrities, and reopens charging three or four times the previous rate for the same rabbit-hutch-sized rooms.

Starck is the man who gets mobbed at the Milan furniture fair, who was called in by Renault to design a special version of the Espace (a project killed off by the company's cash crisis), whose TV sets for Thompson, scales for Teraillon, cigarette lighters for Du Pont, pasta shells, even mineral water bottles and an ashtray are all graced by the Starck scrawl.

What is it that makes the Starck signature such a valuable one to all these clients? Setting to one side the question of talent, there is, first and foremost, the Starck personality itself. He has the kind of quote-worthy charm that would have got him into the headlines even without the famous commission from Mitterand. Starck is like something out of *Diva*. Quirky, but seductively stylish. 'I have a small castle outside Paris. It's completely empty: there's no bed, just a futon on the floor, and a recording studio in the basement. I share it with fifteen friends. Some people call it the zoo, because it's a strange place,' he explains. And it's those kind of qualities which his clients are buying as much as what he actually does for them. They help to explain such curious phenomena as the Philippe Starck ashtray. What else is it that can make a receptacle designed to grind cigarette butts a desirable object? What is on offer is a slice of an undiluted personality: in the increasingly uniform world of industry and mass consumption an ever-rarer commodity.

Starck knows all about the designer star system. He was, after all, on the Pierre Cardin payroll at the tender age of twenty, churning out goodies graced by the then magic name of Cardin. 'I'm interested by the star system. It guarantees you work, and I need that guarantee, I'm a creative junkie, and I have to design every day,' he says.

The power of the Starck name is such that he has even managed to persuade manufacturers to sign contracts with his nine-year-old daughter Ara, whose signature now graces a black rubber stool and will shortly feature on a range of cutlery.

Starck is a natural performer: he knows how to use television, and talks about his relationship with his audience, comparing it, getting only a little carried away, with that of a rock star. It's a seductive but dangerous comparison for a designer. In the old days a half-literate manifesto could keep a competent designer going for his entire career. The designer as star always has to be looking over his shoulder waiting for the next big thing to overtake him. The danger for Starck is that of diminishing returns, of being used up by overexposure. While Starck can reliably be called in to bestow an instant gloss of glamour on anything he touches, he can continue to roam the world in Business Class comfort at 39,000 feet, run an all-black Mercedes, and maintain his château outside Paris.

But when the magic fades – and with a continuous stream of products from pasta shells to lemonade bottles it surely must – he risks the same fall from favour as his predecessor Raymond Loewy.

There are already worrying signs: Starck's attempt to launch his personal version of the Happy Face logo at an exhibition of his work at the Centre Pompidou fell flat. Nobody, it seemed, was particularly interested in buying Starck squiggles on badges and postcards. However, Starck, unlike some designer celebrities, is well aware of the implications of what he is doing. The Pompidou episode, the Ara Starck contracts, all look like deliberate attempts at irony while at the same time exploring the limits of the star system – something like Duchamp's equally unsuccessful attempts to torpedo the art gallery system creating art, by signing ready-mades.

Ferdinand Alexander Porsche represents the opposite end of the spectrum. For a sum that would buy a perfectly respectable car, would-be commandos with an urge to trade in their Gucci loafers for combat boots can purchase the Porsche Design compass watch. Accurate enough to navigate the QE2, it is made from a non-magnetic aluminium alloy so as not to upset the delicate, wafer thin, detachable compass needle hidden behind the face. In the rim of the watch, there is a notch so that you can take directional sightings, and the strap itself can be folded out flat. Each link is exactly 5mm wide, so that you can use it to scale distances on a chart. As standard issue for the SAS it would make a lot of sense, but as a fashion accessory for people whose idea of exercise is to throw away their electric toothbrushes, it does raise a few questions.

In person, the author of all this conspicuous redundancy comes as something of a surprise. He is not the compulsive technophile or the humourless pedant one might expect. Rather, F. A. Porsche has about him something of the air of a monarch in exile. He has a courtly manner: affable and approachable, yet with a certain digni-fied reserve. In blue broadcloth shirt, button-down collar, and suede-patched tweed jacket, he sports a closely trimmed beard, and black signet ring. He drives a Jaguar, and wears an anonymous, but certainly not black, watch. As befits an exiled grandee, he devotes himself to the country. He shoots, he climbs mountains, he looks at the view of the Grossglockner through the all-glass walls of his office in Zell-am-Zee, and he sits and thinks.

The crown prince apparent to one of the most distinguished marques in the world's car industry, Ferdinand Alexander Porsche left the Porsche fief in Stuttgart, gave up any involvement in running the car business, and took himself off to a remote, beautiful corner of Austria, within a stone's throw of the Berchtesgaden.

Rich enough never to have to work again, Porsche deliberately set out to emerge from under the long shadow cast by his grandfather, Alexander the first, the man who created Hitler's people's car.

He runs a studio which employs just six people in Zell-am-Zee, working on everything from portable computers to furniture. He also owns a marketing company, run in tandem with his brother Peter Porsche, that exists to sell a range of products bearing the specific Porsche Design logo, and which in the past ten years has grown from nowhere to become a potential world brand to match the Cartiers and the Dunhills. It is fuelled by an intoxicating mixture of a highly potent name and a ruthlessly severe matt-black aesthetic that runs through everything from sunglasses to wallets.

Powerful though the aura around the Porsche name is, there is also a certain confusion of identity. Porsche products have nothing to do with Porsche cars. Nor is Porsche Design a manufacturer; it works through a combination of licensing and subcontracting. Thus there are some things, such as the sunglasses, which carry both the name of Porsche Design and of Carrera, a name redolent of a Porsche model, which creates still more confusion. And then there are the products designed for other manufacturers which sometimes carry the words 'designed by F. A. Porsche', as in the case of Porsche's Japanese-made telephone.

According to Porsche: 'Twenty to thirty percent of our work is for Porsche Design. We are aware of a certain unclarity over these two directions. The problem is partly a legal one: you can't legally protect the name Porsche Design unless there is actually a company selling products under that name, then there is registered protection. On the other hand the signature designed by F. A. Porsche has no legal protection.'

Porsche admits to being uncomfortable with the aggressive branding of the Porsche name, at its most conspicuous etched like a tattoo across the lenses of the sunglasses which customers as diverse as Yoko Ono and Chuck Yeager are apparently eager to wear. Ono is said to have asked for a $200,000 retainer for endorsing Porsche's Ned Kelly lookalike riveted ski glasses by wearing them so publicly that they have become a personal trademark.

The value of the designer's and the architect's signature is not limited to its association with concrete objects or buildings. The going rate from American Express's advertising agency, Ogilvy and Mather, for an endorsement from a suitably prominent architect is now $25,000. For that the company gets all the kudos of collecting the right architectural names, and none of the fuss of actually having to build anything. And there are plenty of takers. Michael Graves was predictably quick to accept. Ricardo Bofill followed. Richard Rogers refused, but he is the exception which proves the rule. Those who accept American Express's money are then photographed, for what is reputed to be a huge fee, by the fashionable photographer Annie Liebovitz – who ironically refuses to allow her name to be used on the ads – and stare out of magazines proclaiming the bald message 'Card Member since . . .'

For some manufacturers, the value of employing such supposedly illustrious designers lies not so much in the quality of their work, but in the cachet that attaching the right names to their products can bring. There is a story to illustrate the phenomenon at its most extreme. A pencil manufacturer attempted to engage Gae Aulenti, the formidable Italian designer responsible for the transformation of the Gare d'Orsay in Paris into a museum. What it wanted was Aulenti to 'design' a lead pencil. 'But how can I improve on existing pencil designs?' she reportedly objected. 'Oh

Ettore Sottsass made the outrageous colours and the splayed outlines of the Memphis style a worldwide phenomenon, but when it became a high street fashion he found himself in danger of being flattened by the bandwagon he had created

no, you don't actually have to do anything, it's your signature that we want,' came the reply.

Designers may achieve brief periods of fame and fortune, but all too soon find themselves discarded, sucked dry of ideas and individuality, their work exhausted of meaning and content. Hence Ettore Sottsass's anguish a couple of years ago about what he claimed was the disintegration of culture: the way in which fad follows fad, and movement succeeds movement, with an ever-shortening interval between them.

Of course, Sottsass himself was perfectly ready to join the circus of celebrity and media manipulation to get the bandwagon rolling for his Memphis movement. He was always ready to talk to the press, always ready with a good set of slides to ensure maximum publicity. And pretty soon the bandwagon rolled right over him. There are now so-called Memphis apartment towers in New York and Sottsass's unseen presence is co-opted for Carlsberg beer commercials. How would the Bauhaus be seen today, if Walter Gropius had been pictured on the advertising pages of the smart magazines of his day endorsing wine, or Packards?

But then there is nothing really so new about the principle. What has changed is the speed of communication, the rate at which images are used up, and the onslaught of instant nostalgia. If design is what sells things, it becomes vitally important for its continued survival that it can go on selling things. There has to be a fresh supply of image and style to keep up with the ever more sophisticated public taste buds, attuned to every nuance. Otherwise design too could find itself discarded. Already whole countries have suffered this fate. Look at what happened to Denmark. In the 1950s it was the unchallenged leader of the design avant garde. Now it's almost an embarassment, lost in a swamp of antediluvian pine and wholesomeness. What has happened is simple over-harvesting. Too much success in the post-war years stimulated

109

a demand for new design, and, in the end, designers simply ran out of things to say.

Now Italy seems to be heading in the same direction – over-exposure is taking a toll on many of its best-known designers. Hence the sudden rise to prominence of newly discovered groups in Paris and Barcelona, openly challenging Milan's dominance of the design world.

Where design and fashion are still a long way apart, is that fashion has always been used to the idea of fluctuations, but design has not. Fashion is a cyclical affair; changes come according to a well-defined set of rules, oscillating around a set of agreed norms and shared assumptions. Conservatism follows radicalism, sober colours succeed bright ones, hems get longer and then shorter by turns, clothes tighter or looser. Design and architecture, on the other hand, haven't had the time to adjust to playing by these rules. What has been happening over the last five years or so is that an awful lot of material has been completely consumed, used up, and discarded.

As design has come to be seen as more glamorous, it has started to attract the attention of an increasing number of non-designers. The chair, for example, has become a particularly potent medium through which to channel celebrity. The attachment of a key designer's signature can put a huge premium on the price of an otherwise perfectly conventional chair, a phenomenon fuelled by the growth of saleroom prices for 'original' designer pieces. It is a fact that goes some way towards explaining the eagerness with which some manufacturers scour the history books, looking for often justifiably forgotten designs from the masters to put into production as classics with the status of art objects, simply on the strength of the name attached to them. Now furniture makers are even beginning to ask celebrities from other fields to try their hands at design: hence the way in which the Japanese fashion designer Rei Kawakubo now produces chairs, and the decision of the French furniture company XO to commission a chair from Talking Heads' singer, David Byrne.

The phenomenon of the designer and the architect creating signature products is having a curious effect. The transformation of once anonymous objects – telephones, clocks, wristwatches, and so on – is changing the way they are perceived. Once background utility instruments, they are now taking on a much more obvious foreground role.

A piece of furniture that normally nobody would notice is instantly seen differently when it has a name attached to it, a phenomenon uncannily like the sudden shift in perception when a heavily varnished canvas is suddenly identified as being by the hand of an old master. A vivid yellow and green cartoon cut-out cuckoo clock that would be unforgivably kitsch from anyone else is something special, it is implied, when it is created by Robert Venturi.

The company behind this, and other such curious phenomena as the architect-designed wristwatch, is Alessi. The company's history highlights the economic imperatives behind the cult of celebrity. It is very much in the tradition of family-owned Italian companies. Established in the 1920s on the edge of Lake Maggiore, the fourth generation of the Alessi family is now entering the business. It began making simple robust flatware for the catering industry, and did well in international markets, until in the 1970s it found itself increasingly challenged by Far Eastern imports with which it could not compete on price.

Alberto Alessi's stroke of genius was to hit back with products that the Far East could not match: architect-designed artefacts with a visible uniqueness, if that is not a contradiction in terms for a mass-produced object.

It was a move born out of a genuine passion for design on

Alessi's part. And it began in small, highly rarified ways. There was a commission for a group of internationally respected architects, from Arata Isozaki to Oscar Tusquets, to produce a tea service each. Executed in precious metals, and produced on a limited scale, they were more in the nature of an exercise in craft production, and sold at a price and in a style that equated them with fine art. They attracted a lot of attention in the architectural world, but made few ripples outside, beyond a couple of collectors. Then Alessi began to produce its range of kettles by designer names. First there was Richard Sapper – the man who gave the world the praying-mantis Tizio light – who designed a domed creation, with a mournful two-tone steam engine whistle. Then came Michael Graves's kettle, its spout equipped with a red plastic bird, followed by a conical pyramid from Aldo Rossi. Of these, Graves's post-Modern version quickly became the best seller, by a substantial margin. There are cheaper ways to boil water, but that was hardly the point.

Dinner plates, wristwatches, and chairs designed by heavyweight architects are now commonplace. The function of these objects is really immaterial. What counts is their ability to provide the audience with a means of acquiring a slice of the true cross, the work of the master, a shred of his personality. They turn mundane artefacts into works of art – or at least that is the promise.

Alberto Alessi is currently pondering the introduction of Alessi perfumes, a curious full circle that seems to point to the rapid obliteration of all distinction between architecture, design, and fashion. Perfume has traditionally sold on its association with names drawn from the fashion world, but that has been rapidly eroded over the past few years. Why then shouldn't the world's first post-Modernist scent be called Michael Graves? Alessi are working on something suitably metallic.

CHAPTER SIX

ART FOR ART'S SAKE

Nobody was more aware of the impact of celebrity than Andy Warhol, but it was his successors, artists such as Gilbert and George, who went to the extreme of making the lager bottle a work of art, below

When Gilbert and George, two artists who have built their entire careers on presenting themselves as a single seamless personality, held a restrospective exhibition of their work at London's Hayward Gallery last year, they celebrated the event by producing what might, or might not, be called a limited edition. It was a modest enough mixed media work in glass, foil, and metal. Less than seven inches high, it was made for the artists by Beck's Brewery in West Germany. All that distinguished it from every other bottle of Beck's beer sold in Britain by Scottish and Newcastle Breweries was the triple self-portrait emblazoned across the label. The duo appear on three different scales, as photographic fragments, swapping positions and colours to no great effect. Blinking at the camera through his glasses, George, or is it Gilbert, flanks Gilbert, or is it George? Both wear the schoolmasterly houndstooth check suits of curiously retrogarde design that have been their primary means of artistic expression ever since they first met in 1967 as students at St Martin's School of Art. Their dress, and their studiously po-faced expressions, have the curious, and perhaps not entirely unintended, effect of making them look like a couple of television comedians: Morecambe and Wise perhaps.

The label silhouettes them against a black geometric grid in lurid process colours, an effect a little like a stained-glass window. But the reason that this particular work came into being has nothing to do with the traditional preoccupations of art. It adds nothing to our understanding of the human condition, it provides no new insights or perceptions. Instead, it is a direct result of the cut-throat and enormously expensive war that is now being fought for the hearts and minds of British beer drinkers. Scottish and Newcastle, which imports Beck's to Britain, decided that rather than commit itself to spending the £5 million or so it takes to mount an advertising campaign big enough to take on the market

117

leaders, it would move into art sponsorship, very much in the way that cigarette and alcohol companies have traditionally attempted to associate themselves with sport. At just the time that restrictions on promoting alcohol and tobacco are forcing the advertising industry to borrow from the abstract imagery of art, Beck's has attempted to turn its product directly into a work of art.

Working with Anthony Fawcett, one-time secretary to John Lennon and friend of Andy Warhol, now one of a burgeoning army of full-time advisers on the commercial sponsorship of art, Beck's came up with an alternative to saturation advertising exposure. The plan was to create a minority audience for the beer, to make Beck's a cult brand in the hope that a small but influential initial market would in time provide the foundations for a much wider appeal. Opinion formers were targeted directly in the hope that once they were seen drinking Beck's publicly, a much larger group of would-be opinion makers would follow in their footsteps.

Heeding Fawcett's advice, S&N started giving away beer to the organizers of fringe events deemed modish enough to do the brand some good. For a while it became virtually impossible to attend a smart gallery opening or fashion show without tripping over crates of the stuff. The Beck's target customer was seen as being young, fashion conscious, and always on the look-out for something new. 'We saw the Gilbert and George exhibition audience as fitting in with that very well,' says Fawcett. The Hayward exhibition took the whole thing a stage further than sponsorship or endorsement. Rather than simply putting the Beck's logo on the invitations to the private view, the company was able to benefit far more directly. As far as Gilbert and George were concerned, the money helped ensure a bigger and more lavish exhibition than would otherwise have been possible. Beck's, on the other hand, was able to present its product not as just another bottle of beer, but as a work of art in its own right.

118

Two thousand limited edition bottles with the triple self-portrait, along with another six million bottles embellished with an advertising trailer for the exhibition itself, were an overt attempt at enlisting art to turn an everyday object into something special. Of course, Beck's never actually claimed that its bottles were art, it just left you to draw your own conclusions. Was this to be taken seriously as an art work, to be handled with white gloves to preserve the bloom of the colour printing, kept in climate controlled conditions out of direct sunlight, and, of course, never, never to be consumed?

As far as Beck's was concerned, the answer was yes, up to a point at least. Gilbert and George were an ideal choice for the brewers, controversial enough to guarantee that the show got talked about, and tireless enough self-publicists to say yes. The fact that the show was bitterly attacked as meaningless, empty, and distasteful didn't upset their strategy at all. It doesn't seem to have discomforted Gilbert and George much either. They are artists who apparently measure their own worth mainly in terms of column inches of press coverage, these days an increasingly common phenomenon. The catalogue for the Hayward show, its cover decorated by the same triple portrait that appeared on the beer bottle, is accompanied by what purports to be a select bibliography. The densely printed three-page list includes such vital footnotes for future art historians and scholars as Ena Kendall's interesting feature about the duo, 'A Room of My Own', from the *Observer* colour magazine of 10 June 1984, as well as such other useful items as articles from *House and Garden*, the *Daily Mirror*, and *Over 21* magazine. Revealingly, the catalogue is itself full of photographs which show Gilbert and George's works displayed in other museums, presumably to try and prove how important they are.

Quite what the average Hofmeister drinker in the saloon bar

will make of all this is open to doubt. The fact that ordinary lager drinkers will be unlikely even to have heard of Gilbert and George is part of the appeal to those who have. You can't have a cult without outsiders being made to feel put in their place.

Without the extraordinary New York art boom of the 1980s, the Beck's campaign would have been unthinkable. Of course, art had always exuded a certain glamour, even if an awful lot of the avant-garde spent most of its time right up until the 1950s and after getting unfashionably malnourished in New York lofts and Paris attics. But around the time that Julian Schnabel, leader of the art brat pack, had his unprecedented two-gallery show at the Castelli and Mary Boone galleries in 1981, and Keith Haring emerged from the nether regions of Manhattan's Danceteria Club, where he had been happily whiling away the odd hour graffiting the walls in the cloakroom, things began to change. Fuelled by a massive injection of new money made on the great Wall Street bull market, and the dizzying prices that the New York school led by Jasper Johns were commanding, art suddenly became very chic indeed.

Artists were now being photographed for society magazines, they gave up starving and were to be found instead lunching at the smarter restaurants. Suddenly they could join the gravy train. A crop of artists, or would-be artists, had been able to get rich with remarkable ease. Piet Mondrian had been broke at thirty. Brian Clarke was employing a secretary and a personal assistant at the same point in his career. Yet unlike their predecessors, the popular salon artists of the nineteenth century, who were also not short of the material rewards of life, the Schnabels and the Scharfs were able to go on presenting themselves as outlaws.

In the old days, way back in 1977, smart New York night-life had centred on the fashion names. Calvin Klein and Halston, along

Kenny Scharf, according to his enthusiastic clients at the Villa Zapu wine company, is one of America's most brilliant contemporary artists. His work can be found at the Mudd Club, the Palladium, and on Zapu wine labels

with clients like Bianca Jagger, held court at Steve Rubell's Studio 54, safe from the sweaty crush at the door. Now it was suddenly the art names – not just the painters, but the dealers and the collectors too – who were the most heavily fashionable tourist attractions, the ones who drew the swivelling radar eyes in the clubs and restaurants. Steve Rubell, his tenure at Studio 54 interrupted by difficulties over an income tax bill that led to a spell in a minimum security facility, lived to ride another day with the Palladium, the club which he did his best to fill knee-deep in art and artists.

The Palladium's interior was designed by Arata Isozaki, the most fashionable Japanese export since raw fish. Isozaki was putting the finishing touches to the new Los Angeles Museum of Contemporary Art at about the same time, a highly satisfactory coincidence for Rubell. The club had a Francesco Clemente mural on top of the stairs, and Kenny Scharf in the telephone booths. Unfortunately, what it did not have for very long was the smart crowd, who took off down to Nell's as soon as it became clear that the Palladium was just too big for its own good, too large to be truly exclusive, and then skipped to MK's.

But despite regular tongue lashings from Robert Hughes, scourge of graffiti art and self-promoting neo-expressionists, the new breed of artists as celebrities continued to flourish. It wasn't just the club-goers who were interested in the social value of art. In a remarkable piece in *Vanity Fair*, Doris Saatchi – herself one of the most voracious collectors of the new art, thanks to her husband and fellow collector Charles Saatchi's advertising fortune – quoted the doyen of the New York gallery owners, Leo Castelli. 'For someone who has a lot of money and wants to participate in the big world, the best thing they could do is set up a great collection.' Art was the passport to social acceptability, the ticket to the smart openings, the black tie dinners, and the warm bath of self-esteem that comes from those tiny words 'from the collection of . . .' in the catalogue to the hot new show in town.

Doris outlined her succinct view of contemporary art in the course of what was ostensibly a piece on the New York taxi-cab millionaire Robert Scull, and the record-breaking sale of his collection of post-war American art. 'If contemporary art were baseball, the artist who would be Babe Ruth and Hank Aaron in one, the heavy hitter, the home run king of his day, is hands down, no contest, Jasper Johns,' she wrote, an analogy that, taken to its logical conclusion, would reduce the Saatchi collection to a set of bubblegum cards.

What had attracted her admiration was the fact that a Jasper Johns had sold at the Scull sale in 1986 for a breathtaking $3.6 million, then the highest price ever achieved by a contemporary artist. At the same sale another Johns that had failed to reach its reserve at auction back in 1973, when the bidding stopped at $105,000, went for $1.7 million. They were the kind of figures that made art headline news and turned the sale rooms into highly charged gladiatorial arenas, in which the collectors themselves could share a little of the glory. After all, what is painting a $3.6 million canvas compared with paying for it, especially when, if you are smart enough, you can watch your investment appreciate tenfold in a decade? No wonder that the really big bids now attract gasps and rounds of well-bred applause in the sale rooms.

The tone is set by winking electronic currency conversion boards hanging over the auction floors, and the telephone bids from Tokyo. It's not as if any art world tycoon worth his salt isn't equipped with his own perfectly serviceable Braun calculator. The scoreboards are there to add a little melodrama, to give the players a sense of occasion. At this rate, collecting could soon be taking centre stage over painting.

The sheer scale of the money involved has transformed the

nature of the art business. In 1958 Sotheby's sales were $16 million, last year they reached $1.3 billion. The company prints 400 different catalogues a year, which go to its 75,000 regular subscribers, the hard core of the new breed of collectors.

Perhaps none of this is so different from the patronage of those fourteenth-century Italian merchant bankers, the Medicis. But then the artist had yet to acquire the boundless vanity of the present, and, equally, part of the point of signing up the imprimatur of an artist is to say, subtly or otherwise, that yes, we are the modern Medicis. Museums and their architecture are specifically intended to encourage all this. More and more they are designed not for the optimum presentation of the works in them, but, as in the case of the I.M. Pei extension at the Washington National Gallery, to provide a suitable backdrop for star-struck parties, or to allow patrons to add to their own reputation by endowing wings.

The museum is the ultimate opportunity for the social aggrandizement of the collector. To have a wing of a museum named after you is the path to immortality on the cheap. In America, at least, supine curators fall over themselves to accept the terms of bequests which specify that works hang exactly as they did in the benefactor's suburban living room, and that the walls are decorated in the same wallpaper. Walk around New York's Metropolitan Museum, and you see one after another of these grisly phenomena. It all feels like the Monumental Cemetery in Milan, where family tombs, outdoing each other in ostentation and sentimentality, vie for the greater glory of their own family names.

The museum sanctifies all it touches, even the most mundane of products. Carl André's off-the-shelf bricks straight from the builder's yard would have been completely impossible outside a museum context. Looked at in the most materialistic of terms, art

123

is the fastest and most effective value-adding operation imaginable. What else allows you to pick up a paint brush and convert £50 worth of canvas and paint into a museum-quality work immediately worth £30,000?

But even more than this, art museums transform the names of those associated with them, those who finance them, and those whose work hangs in them, because, of course, the signature attached to that £50 worth of canvas and paint is of such crucial importance. All of which is exactly the same kind of equation that prompts Armani to put his name on telephones and Cardin to stamp his signature on colognes.

With art assuming such vital social roles, there is less and less top quality merchandise to go around. To feed the burgeoning demand, says Doris Saatchi, 'Artists must now work on an almost industrial scale, high culture is adapting its output to the consumer society.' Despite the panic-buying tactics that characterize the Saatchis' collecting style, there is not a sign of her tongue being in her cheek.

The primary manifestation of that adaptation is the vastly increased number of aspiring artists, the legions of easily recognized and facile celebrity artists – the Keith Harings, Kenny Scharfs, and the rest of the graffitists. You can see the hunger for art celebrities in the Rose's Lime Juice advertising campaign. The company took costly space in a range of glossy magazines carefully targeted at the opinion formers. One of the series of ads they ran is largely devoted to a photograph of an unknown young man. He wears a white t-shirt and white-painted, hobnailed boots. From the paint and the canvas in the background, we can safely assume that he is an artist, clearly not long into his twenties. The black leather jacket he wears is, however, new, paid for perhaps with the substantial cheque he will have received from Rose's to appear in the photograph. In eight-point type, printed white on white, and barely visible even with a magnifying glass, is the identifying legend, James Mather. Here is the commercial exploitation of dawn-fresh, dew-picked charisma before it has even become celebrity. So hip are the Rose's Lime Juice crowd, implies the ad, that once the rest of the world has heard of its idols, then they are too old hat for words.

The grandfather of all this is Andy Warhol, who began by exploring the icons of popular culture, and ended up by turning himself into one. Andy Warhol was perfectly happy to take a liquor company's money to produce a work that appeared in millions of magazines over the bold headline 'Absolut Warhol'. Indeed, Warhol also endorsed a range of other products, including Pontiac cars, Pioneer hi-fi, Château Mouton Rothschild, and the merchant bankers Drexel Burnham Lambert. The Campbell soup company, of course, had his services for nothing. But that was a very different exercise. In his commercial phase, Warhol was simply selling his services to the highest bidder in an attempt to change the way the world saw their products. He had begun with the vastly more radical undertaking of challenging the way in which art was perceived, by exploring the power of banal commercial images. Towards the end of his career, Warhol couldn't go anywhere without somebody emerging from the crowd, pulling a can of chicken soup from a back pocket, and asking Andy to sign it. Andy was, of course, only too happy to oblige.

Warhol never flinched from addressing the intimate links between art and business. Beneath the irony, he was perfectly open about it. His magazine *Interview*, for example, eschewed all forms of editorial intervention. Its journalism took the form of pointing a tape-recorder at the subject and transcribing the results. He was unabashed at using the magazine to sell the idea of commissioning a Warhol portrait.

Sweden's Absolut Vodka company hired not only Warhol but Scharf and Haring, below, to design advertisements adding a touch of culture, or so it hoped, to its product

ABSOLUT HARING.

Warhol spent his whole career exploring the contradictions between the fetish for the original image and its mechanical reproduction. But whatever his intentions, he ended up as one of the twentieth century's most potent art brand names, with an audience perfectly happy to pay for the privilege of owning a Warhol Polaroid, or even a Warhol Xerox. Within months of his death, Warhol's executor had sold rights to the commercial exploitation of his name on a scale that even Warhol hadn't achieved in his lifetime. The Swiss watch company Movado is bringing out the Warhol watch, and Warhol cards and stationery are not far behind.

What all these uses of art and artists have in common is that they focus on the artist himself. His personality, or projected personality, is much more important than the work.

Warhol became famous through his work, then created himself as a personality. Tyros such as Mather have their personalities as celebrities created for them by Rose's advertising agency. Gilbert and George, or even Joseph Beuys, project themselves, in the former's case without much of an ironical edge, using the same high-visibility techniques as any other aspiring celebrity. With Warhol there was his trademark wig. Beuys adopted a permanent uniform of fishing jacket and trilby. Gilbert and George go even further, and always wear exactly the same clothes for their appearances – though performances might be a better word.

Keith Haring went so far as to open the Pop Shop which sells his vacuous 'art' merchandise, on a par with Michael Jackson lunch buckets. Apologists for Haring present his work as dealing with the imagery of popular culture, and the manipulative forces behind it. But as the forensic work of Hans Haacke shows, there are other, more convincing, ways of dealing with the imagery of consumer society than simply by joining it.

Too often there are alarmingly close parallels between the way that artistic careers progress, and the marketing of a product.

126

Artists too develop corporate identities, making their work immediately recognizable to their audience. So it is that Gilbert and George's flat vivid portraits, or Julian Schnabel's smashed plates, assure their customers that they have acquired the genuine article, and, of course, they can display them to their friends confident that the label will be recognizable on their walls.

Perhaps this is an inevitable consequence of the way in which the artist himself has become the focus of attention. It is the retrospective which has become the show that all painters want: Schnabel got his before he was thirty. In this they have become just like fashion designers who insist their backers provide ego-boosting shops that carry their names, rather than let them take their chances in the hurly burly of department stores.

The fetish for the signature is what has triggered off the whole phenomenon. It embodies the romantic myth of artistic creation, the feeling that artists are, in some undefined sense, not as other men are. That their touch turns base merchandise into something other-worldly. The problem is that most artists *are* exactly as other men are, and that they are all too happy to make a quick profit. Salvador Dali might conceivably have been able to argue that his intentions were basically subversive when he allowed his name to be sold to a cosmetics company. His licensees went as far as turning one of his squiggles into a bottle. The 'limited edition crystal flacon', as they insist on calling it, is a bottle in the form of a pair of surrealist lips, with a Daliesque nose for a stopper, which will set you back £1,750. The irony, if that is what it is, is likely to escape the customers. Certainly it's one which went whistling over the head of *Elle* magazine which, without a trace of a smile, reported that, 'inspired by the success of his perfume, Dali has created a fragrance for men in woody rustic and amber tones'. Prices for the Dali deodorant start at a mere £9.95.

Dali originally set out to shock the bourgeosie, but ended up collaborating in selling it cologne. Surely the genuine surrealist's perfume would smell of rotten eggs?

CHAPTER SEVEN

FACE THE MUSIC

Elvis, immortalized by Warhol, and Ché Guevara provided the role models for the slenderized George Michael in his solo career

George Michael is caught in the beam of what appears to be the landing light of a jumbo jet, trained directly at the top of his skull. Five thousand lux blaze down through atmospheric clouds of smoke and dust, turning his carefully streaked and moulded hair into a neat rectangular halo. One hand is punched high up over his shoulder, in a gesture of aimless defiance. In the other he grips a radio mike.

Since technological obsolescence put an end to the dominance of the guitar, the microphone has become the essential prop for an aspiring rock star. Stunted high-tech guitars made of plastic make attempts to emulate the pyrotechnics of Pete Townshend look as risible as the Coldstream Guards drilling with miniature modern rifles. Hence the importance of the mike, freed at last from the shackles of a stand. Some are designed as headsets, strapped in place to allow vocalists prepared to go on stage looking like air traffic controllers to indulge in frenzied outbursts of unfettered, hands-free emoting. But Michael's is of the more macho, hand-held variety: matt black, and with a pistol grip like a Beretta.

Michael wears jeans that have clearly been frayed by experts, a belt as big as a spare tyre, and a white vest of the type once favoured for their leading men by social realist theatre directors attempting to signify proletarian authenticity. The look is Spartacus meets Ché Guevara. Taken at face value, it is a trifle far-fetched for a singer who is the product of prosperous north London suburbia, especially one with a $10 million sponsorship contract with a Japanese electronics company in his pocket. But then music should never be taken entirely at face value.

Post-Wham, George Michael has sharpened up his image, getting to grips with an incipient weight problem. His act mixes the two conflicting impulses – to outrage and to succeed – that have shaped pop music. He uses the trappings of youthful rebellion to give an edge to his winsome glamour. His pose has been carefully constructed as part of the marketing effort for his new album. And it expertly recycles imagery from a variety of sources to create an identity that quickly takes on an independent existence. Conspicuously lacking in menace, but amply endowed with charm, Michael is the apotheosis of the rock star as entertainer. He is as much a part of popular culture as Charlie Chaplin or the music hall stars once were. Michael's success represents a remarkable transformation of the music industry. In the 1950s and 60s fashionable music was the preserve of rebel rockers, outlaw heroes to the newly discovered *genus* teenager, folk devils to adults driven to paroxysms of moral panic at the prospect of jungle music sweeping all before it.

The young Elvis Presley, sounding like a black man and looking blatantly sexual, was every red-neck nightmare come true. He opened the flood gates of permissiveness that allowed Chuck Berry, Little Richard, and a host of other blacks onto previously all-white radio stations, and thence into the charts. His bruised lips and blue-black quiff were painted by Andy Warhol, and, after Presley's death, became the stigmata of a quasi-religious cult that was scarcely diminished by revelations of barbiturate and junk food binges.

Despite the best efforts of Elvis's manager, Colonel Parker, the traditional slickness and glitz that had characterized music business professionalism suddenly became a joke. Marooned on the wrong side of the generation gap, music entrepreneurs were temporarily baffled about what was happening, as they were meant to be. All the ins suddenly turned into outs. The quickest, most effective way to make a unilateral declaration of independence from the grown-up world was to elevate conspicuously to hero status a band of musicians who apparently embodied contempt for everything that their elders held dear. Both sides of the age divide briefly got carried away, and behaved as if there was real substance to all the Oedipean symbolism. For the tabloid press, publicity-conscious clergymen, and the more simple minded of pundits, the young started to look very menacing indeed. But far from representing a revolutionary vanguard, rock and roll turned out to be just another sunrise industry, one that produced at least as many new millionaires as computers did a decade later. And whatever their enthusiasm for narcotics, bourbon, and groupies, most of them share the comfortable values of successful self-made men the world over. The survivors take up polo, play at being gentleman farmers, and have their shoes hand made in Jermyn Street. In the last decade, enterprise culture has overtaken the cheerful anarchy of the early days of rock; and musical outrage has become increasingly ritualized. George Michael's clenched fist cheerfully acknowledges the triumph of form over substance.

Musicians like Michael look the way they do, because that is the way rock stars are meant to look. Nobody professes to believe that music will change the world anymore, but appearances are still important. The lonesome outsider caught in the spotlight is the superstar ideal. And George Michael's poor boy get-up is part of the traditional rock star act. It harks back to a golden age of interminable drum solos and patchouli for its legitimacy. In the same way that the founding fathers of the fledgling republic of the United States of America were forever having themselves painted and sculpted wearing the togas of republican Rome as a testament to their evaluation of their own worth, so popular music keeps on referring back to its own past.

Showmanship, the other strand to popular music, is equally important. With no cultural pretensions, it draws on the tradition of slick black performers dating back to the Tamla Motown label, and the white bubblegum pop of the same period. It's an approach to music that grew out of the sequin-stitched style of the circus, and puts a premium on glamour and entertainment. Michael, a true *pop* star, is a natural inheritor of the tradition.

Ruffle for ruffle, Prince re-creates the stage presence of Jimi Hendrix

It's very noticeable how many of the current crop of stars depend on the myths that surround the heroes of rock's glory days. But though they may look like them, the edge of danger has gone. Prince, with his peace sign medallions and his overtly sexual stage performance, could not have existed without Jimi Hendrix. Yet despite being considerably more provocative, he has never engendered the same kind of outrage that Hendrix did in the late 1960s. Hendrix was treated like the demon king of rock and roll, flouting sexual and racial taboos, but at least he kept his clothes on. Prince, on the other hand, is pictured stark naked in a thousand high street record shop windows, lubriciously flaunting his androgynous physique. But far from being seen as a threat to civilization as we know it, he is treated as a loveable eccentric, even by Rupert Murdoch's notoriously vicious gossips, and gets himself photographed lining up for a Big Mac in McDonalds to show what a regular guy he is. Similarly, homespun New Jersey populist Bruce Springsteen draws on the traditions of Bob Dylan and an earlier generation of radical balladeers, but ends up being quoted with approval by Ronald Reagan.

The changing status enjoyed by musicians is graphically demonstrated by the way that the press have adopted them as an essential part of their repertoire, along with television soap stars, snooker players, and royalty. When the Rolling Stones started playing in the cellars of Richmond a quarter of a century ago, it would have been unthinkable for the quality newspapers to review their performances. *The Times* provoked derision on the one occasion in the 1960s when it did take the Beatles' talents as songwriters seriously. Now, it's not just the culturally respectable old war horses like the Stones, with honorary Frank Sinatra status as legends in their own lifetime, who get coverage in the heavies – it is the teenybop idols too.

The tabloids once relished portraying rock musicians as antisocial deviants. Now they are followed with the same enthusiasm as television stars, and their characters are depicted with the same childishly violent swings of mood. Occasionally they are elevated to the saintlike status of Bob Geldof; at other times – witness the sad treatment of Elton John by the *Sun* – they are turned over in the interests of boosting circulation. Either way, it is taken for granted that it is not just the record-buying young who are interested in their doings. The status of music columnists in the British newspaper hierarchy has shot up accordingly. While coverage of sports stars, apart from the occasional tennis tantrum or cricketing outrage, is usually confined to the back pages, music names regularly make front page news.

The press often delights in the very ordinariness of celebrities. When the Princess of Wales forgets to take her purse on a shopping trip to buy a sweater at Benetton, the tabloids erupt in a frenzy of headlines. Similarly, when Michael Jackson demonstrates the same hunger pangs as the rest of us, and interrupts the regal progress of his motorcade across the countryside to halt at a motorway cafe for his flunkeys to buy chocolate, it is *news*.

The press is never more delighted than when it can indulge in celebrity matchmaking: former EastEnders star Anita Dobson sent the tabloids into ecstacy when she took up with a rock musician. And it takes particular pleasure in mixing music with television. The curious phenomenon of Kylie Minogue, the Australian soap star who began her recording career by covering hits from the 1950s, is seized on with relish. Samantha Fox's records are treated with the same enthusiasm, making it clear just how poor a second musical abililty comes to a high public profile in chart success. Such performers stand in the same relationship to the music business that certain of the more mature film stars do to the perfume makers. They are in demand for the appeal of their names to a particular segment of the market.

The press and the music business enjoy a two-way relationship. Fledgling musicians are pathetically anxious to do anything to get every plug, photograph, and paragraph in print they can to help launch their careers – an anxiety that diminishes if and when their careers do take off. With success, they typically adopt a tone of disdainful hauteur, deigning to speak to the press only on the eve of tours or album releases. In the early stages of their careers, they make willing and eager participants on the celebrity bandwagon, employing the services of press agents who, for a fee, will arrange for their clients to be photographed in restaurants in close physical proximity with more famous personalities. Yet all the attention has the curious effect of diminishing the status of music stars. It may make their names and faces more familiar, but instead of presenting their images only in the carefully choreographed setting of a live performance, or the hermetic context of a recording or video, they are revealed in day-by-day close-up in all their ordinariness. Just like royalty, music stars have responsibilities to their public. The fanzines reserve the right to ridicule their idols, as well as to worship them. The essential subtext of hagiography is that they are, after all, *our* creations, ours to admire, and to destroy.

The mystery disappears still more quickly when the advertising industry co-opts music wholesale. Music is used relentlessly for commercial ends. Levis, in particular, mount loving re-creations of the great days of rock and roll, for an audience that is far too young to remember them at first hand. Heavy metal soundtracks from the more recent past are used on TV commercials to hint none too subtly that a sensible family saloon needn't sink the young-at-heart self-image of the balding middle manager with two children and a mortgage, who clearly does remember the Isle of Wight Pop Festival, but wishes he was too young to have been there. Music and advertising are locked in an incestuous

Malcolm McLaren turned the anarchy of Johnny Rotten, or John Lydon as he prefers to be called now, into a highly successful corporate identity

embrace. Advertising sells not only the product, but also the music that it uses for its soundtracks. The fading career of a many a retired star has been given an unexpected boost by the recycling of their early hits as soundtracks on commercials. One result is that those who still seek to recapture the authentic flavour of outrage of the early stars have had to resort to bizarre extremes that border on self-parody. Simply biting the heads off chickens isn't enough any more, as the picturesquely named Revolting Cocks discovered: they adorn their albums with the images of hard core pornography. More genuinely threatening are the American rap bands, such as Public Enemy, who foster an atmosphere of violent menace around their performances, so much so that in Britain, at least, some stadium managers have been reluctant to allow them to use their premises for live perform-ances. It has yet to be seen whether they are ready to soften their stand in the interests of long-term financial security.

The lastingly successful performers, in economic terms at least, follow broadly similar career trajectories, initially establishing themselves with a given subculture, then extending that original appeal to a general audience. The Sex Pistols managed the first half of that strategy brilliantly. Under the Svengali-like influence of Malcolm McLaren they virtually invented the punk movement. But the second stage was beyond them. And like so many old troopers who go on touring when their careers start to slide, they found themselves slipping back into the embrace of a diminishing, rigidly self-defined audience.

Even the most famous names of the 1960s began their careers appealing to a ghetto audience. Jagger and the Rolling Stones were once the preferred musicians of the first generation of grammar school boys to wear hair over their collars. Pete Town-shend and the Who played the same role for cropped, scooter-riding mods. But an example with probably more relevance for the present day is the Bay City Rollers. In their day they were the subject of as much hero worship as the Rolling Stones. The difference is that they carried an appeal with less longevity, for a tribe with rather less elevated social ambitions than the Stones. They nevertheless provided a ready-made identity for a group of adolescents looking for the security and reassurance of belonging. For the Bay City Roller clones of 1973, in their improbable platform soles, their page-boy haircuts, their braces, and grotesque tartan-fringed baggy trousers, just as for the Brosettes of 1988, in their suede pilot's jackets, curious lace-up boots, and peroxide crops, the function of the music hero is a tribal one. To be able to project a recognizable persona, or an insignia, capable of being readily adopted by fans, is crucial for an aspiring musician. The Beastie Boys, with their VW radiator badges round their necks, were spectacularly successful, as countless thousands of irate car owners will testify. The two primary elements that the image makers have to play with are hair and clothes. There are two natural extremes: the tatters and flowing locks of the heavy metal looser on the one hand, and the carefully pressed suit and short back and sides of the Rick Astleys on the other. In between, a rich variety of possibilities is on offer.

A marketable image can be a simple accentuation of an already existing look: the Jam kitted themselves out as mods, to become the standard bearers of the mod revival. Or it can be the complete creation, from scratch, of a new style that has followers rushing off to adopt it wholesale. That is why the music business has proved such fertile ground for the merchandisers. The followers identify with their tribe by dressing like their idols, by buying all kinds of products that carry their motif.

Celebrity has never been more vital to the music world. The constant ebb and flow of the temporarily bright new names demonstrates just how carefully fame must be nurtured for the ageing music industry to stay healthy. Many record companies now have stock-market listings which depend for their continued appeal in the City on a constant supply of fresh new stars, just as an oil company must go on prospecting. Following the pattern set by the brewers and the petrol companies who own the pubs and garages that they supply, music industry hardware manufacturers like Sony are busy acquiring the software too. Sony, the most technologically inventive of the Japanese audio equipment manufacturers, bought up the CBS record business, neatly closing a circle and marking an important step forward in its battle to control every aspect of the music cycle. A TV station would be the logical next step. Given such a development it is hardly surprising that music is now seen as an industrial process: one in which raw product is processed and exploited. The technical end of the business can be left safely in the hands of the expert producers. Stock, Aitken, and Waterman are only the most recent in a long line of reliable hit makers. And productivity in the recording studio is rising rapidly thanks to sophisticated instruments that can synthesize rythmns with a little deft switch throwing. The image-creating end of the business, essential to shifting adequate quantities of product, is now coming in for the greatest input of technological investment and creative effort. It's at this level that the musician as hero is so important. The rock stars of the 1960s were presented as super heroes with gargantuan appetites, both carnal and narcotic. Without all the videos and the choreography, the current crop of stars would look decidely pale by comparison. Their sexual exploits, and occasional heroin addictions, are decidedly unheroic now that exactly the same vices, stripped of glamour, are reaching epidemic proportions.

The universal adoption of the video as a tool of the music business has helped to lessen dependence on musical ability for success, at least in the short term, and to quicken the pace of the musical fashion cycle. The rock video attracts a level of investment and calculation that matches the recording itself. And as a medium for conveying a mood and an image it is unmatched in its power. Since round-the-clock music channels began broadcasting on American television, the rock video has been crucial to selling records. And to service the constant appetite for fresh imagery, art history has been ransacked by the rock video directors. Image makers like Malcolm McLaren, with an art school background, have become crucial. He masterminded Adam Ant's war-paint pirate look, before beginning his own career in the recording studio. Major film directors are now also becoming involved: Ken Russell, for one, has a string of rock videos under his belt. And Andy Warhol's studio shot a video for the English band, Curiosity Killed the Cat. The Pet Shop Boys, leery of testing the attractions of their charms in front of a big audience, went as far as making a feature length film. But that is exceptional. The three-minute video is the norm, and amounts to an extended TV commercial for a band in which the main selling point is the celebrity of the individual attached to it. Sometimes there are other products on offer under the same brand image. Run DMC, for example, have a line of footwear licensed to Adidas.

Ultimately it is the international audience that matters economically. It is still the traditional markets of Britain and America that set the pace in style terms, and that produce the vast majority of the international stars. However, the reason that records by today's music stars so effortlessly outsell those of the superstars of the 1960s is the vastly larger record-buying audience for rock in the Far East, Africa, and Latin America. Clearly, tailoring the performers to appeal to a wider range of tastes is important.

At the same time, the whole business has become more and

The Goss brothers, otherwise known as Bros, are keen on looking tough. But manager Tom Watkins – previously a designer with Terence Conran – knows best when it comes to selling the group

more a self-conscious commercial opportunity. Investors, managers, and producers prospecting for likely raw material now look as much for visual presence, and the requisite degree of exhibitionism, as for musical experience. Today's teeny band is only the tip of an elaborate commercial network of investors, managers, agents, and publishers, as is revealed graphically by the court case fought by Holly Johnson, formerly of Frankie Goes to Hollywood, with his record company ZTT. In court, ZTT argued that they had created the group hits, with minimal involvement from the Frankies. The judge, however, ruled that Johnson should be released from his contract as it constituted what he called an unfair restraint of trade. It was a revealing, if brutally frank, way of describing what has always politely been presented as an art.

Reports of similarly unsavoury dealings have emerged in connection with the formation of Curiosity Killed the Cat, a group named and launched by a life insurance salesman whose management contract gave him twenty per cent of their earnings in exchange for arranging to fund them for the year it took to sign their first recording contract.

As an economic path out of the dole queues, music is now a well-trodden route. But the nuances of taste dividing generations are such that today's musical blockbuster is quickly designated as nostalgia as a succeeding wave of younger brothers and sisters consign their elder siblings' idols to the musical scrap heap. 'When will I be famous?' ask Bros, matching blondes in trying-to-be-tough leather jackets, doing their best to adopt a confident sneer. Meanwhile, thousands of schoolgirls flood the pages of the fanzines, recounting their desperate attempts to meet the trio. When they talk about going to the delirious lengths of writing to the Duchess of York, asking her to intercede, it is clear that this really is the age of celebrity, and that music is still close to the top of the hierarchy.

Gloria Vanderbilt
Gloria Vanderbilt
Gloria Vanderbilt
Gloria Vanderbilt
Gloria Vanderbilt

CHAPTER EIGHT

THE PERILS OF INFLATION

Halston kissed his career as an exclusive designer goodbye when he sold his name to a multinational that put him into chain stores and lost him couture clients such as Liza Minelli

If Datsun or Ford ever managed to take over Rolls-Royce and the Spirit of Ecstasy found herself undignifiedly impaled on the bonnets of a range of upper mid-market saloons, the resulting cars would, no doubt, enjoy a certain appeal. There certainly *is* an audience that would be keen on the idea of driving behind a Rolls radiator for the price of a Granada. How loyal an audience it would be is another matter. For the first couple of seasons the new regime could make quick profits, cashing in on the premium that the Rolls name carries. But the Rolls cachet, and the value of the name, would quickly go into steep decline as it became abundantly clear that Rolls-Royce just wasn't Rolls-Royce anymore. There are those who would say that *any* association with the mass market would taint the marque beyond recovery, but the experience of Mercedes Benz, which has successfully produced a budget car without losing its allure for the ambassadorial classes, suggests otherwise. The skilful operator can pull off the difficult feat of playing both ends of the market at once. The less adroit plunge into the chasm between the two. Their names, far from bestowing a patina of desirability, become an embarrassment.

It's a problem that is already facing Rolls, though for different reasons. The original meaning of its name, shorthand for thorough-bred English engineering excellence, has already been eclipsed by the kind of people who actually drive Rollers these days. Plastering the Rolls name all over sunglasses, key rings, and coffee mugs would only help the process along. Yet this is exactly the strategy that those in possession of other once equally illustrious names have recklessly attempted. Burberry, for one, with its tartan snowstorm of Burberry-labelled knick-knackery, has taken this course, and it's one that can do the long-term future of the company's classic raincoat very little good.

The career of André Courrèges, one-time civil engineer, pupil of the great Balenciaga, and sometimes credited as the inventor of the mini skirt, is a salutory warning of what happens when people set about exploiting a good name over-enthusiastically. In the early 1960s, after he had first opened up his own couture salon in Paris, Courrèges quickly became the most celebrated name in the fashion world. His ice-pink, white, and silver mannequins, wandering about like lost robots in their giant silver sunglasses and metal foil swimsuits, set the tone for a novelty-fixated decade. Courrèges was the antithesis of nostalgia with his glossy patent leather stripes, his ribbed jersey cosmonaut bodystockings, and those curious cut-out origami white leather boots that became a uniform for the chic but wealthy of the 1960s. Lee Radziwill, Margaret Trudeau, and Princess Ira von Furstenburg all swallowed the Courrèges line.

Vogue called him 'as refreshing as a streak of luck,' and gave him saturation coverage. Courrèges made fashion into headline news, playing on his notoriety with a series of *succès de scandale* convention-flouting styles. But despite putting women in trousers at a time when a whole generation of maître d's still professed to find this shocking, and cutting skirts to four inches above the knee, Courrèges was still in the outstandingly conventional business of selling hand-made one-off clothes to the rich, a contradiction that was to be his downfall. He began to lose his way in the 1970s, when he failed to bring off the difficult feat of simultaneously juggling a couture house and a chain of mass-market boutiques. The Hyperbole ready-to-wear line, a fur range, and the Sports Futur sportswear collection all blurred into one with the top-of-the-range couture clothes. Worse, the Courrèges Barbarella look was dating badly.

Things went seriously wrong in the 1980s, reaching a nadir in 1985 when Courrèges couldn't afford to put on a Paris collection at all, an omission that led to his expulsion from the Chambre Syndicale. L'Oreal, the cosmetics company that had acquired the rights to his name, had already decided that it had wrung Courrèges dry of every ounce of prestige that it could and that there was nothing to be gained from holding on to Eau de Courrèges. They sold Courrèges on to Itokin, his Japanese distributors, who, with grim-faced determination, are now busy flogging the name to death. In Japan, the knacker's yard for time-expired celebrities, a European cachet is still very important, so the Courrèges logo is applied to everything in sight, from telephones to cameras, clearly with no more involvement from the unhappy designer than the application of the name that he can no longer call his own. Once Courrèges personified modern chic, now he is hopelessly *démodé*, and unfortunately his name is precisely the one that the fashion conscious do not want to carry about on their possessions.

Halston, once America's best-known fashion designer, ended up losing control of his name in an equally dismal fall from grace. He now finds himself highly paid not to produce at all, an employee of a company that owns his name but which isn't interested in him creating anything just at the moment.

Halston was the first of America's celebrity designers. Born Roy Halston Frowick, he shed the outer appendages to his name to emerge with the suitably magisterial single moniker. In his glory days, he was the Hollywood art director's dream of a fashion designer. His palatial New York office, with its orchids and its blood red carpet woven with his initials, staffed by squads of monochrome assistants, looked like updated Busby Berkeley. He dressed Lauren Bacall, Liza Minelli, and Bianca Jagger, among others. It was Halston who kitted Jackie Kennedy out with her trademark pillbox hat.

In 1973, Halston signed a deal with Norton Simon Inc., a sprawling multinational which owned, apart from the Max Factor cosmetics company, the Avis car rental business. For between $12 and $16 million, Norton Simon acquired the Halston trademark, control of his couture and ready-to-wear operations, and the right to put his name on just about any product they chose. Max Factor launched the Halston scent and it remains one of America's best-sellers, in its Elsa Peretti bottle. What triggered his downfall was Norton Simon's decision to put the Halston name on a series of collections to be sold 'exclusively' by the deeply unfashionable J. C. Penney department store chain. The deal no doubt did J. C. Penney a lot of good in upgrading their image, but for Halston it was a disaster. As soon as the J. C. Penney contract was made public Bergdorf Goodman, the store that gave Halston his first chance to design clothes and had loyally supported him for twenty years, announced that they would be dropping him. Why would their customers be interested in buying the products of a designer from their exclusive fashion floor, when they could find them in any chain store up and down the country?

Soon after, Norton Simon was itself taken over, and ownership of Halston's name went through five different companies in less than four years. By 1986, Halston belonged to Revlon. The couture operation had been closed down, and the designer sat at home unable to put his name on anything without Revlon's approval, his unhappiness hardly mollified by being able to collect a salary reportedly in six figures – a price which Revlon were happy to pay, given the money they were continuing to make out of Halston's fragrances.

It isn't just the fashion world which has been churning out disposable celebrities. Pop has always been a revolving door, through which celebrities move in and out with alarming predict-ability. In the nature of things, the Bay City Rollers or the Monkees, Duran Duran or Bananarama, and groups like them, often have a very short shelf life. Not surprisingly their managers and record companies have always tried to cash in as hard and as quickly as they could, treating their audiences as the children that they are, using hit-and-run tactics to maximize their earning power in the brief period of attention they have, and putting out every kind of trashy poster and licensing deal that they could think of.

The music business's problem is its lack of staying power. Partly it's to do with the speed with which the system sucks in new talent, turns it into star material, then spits it out again as old hat. But it's also due to the sad fact that a lot of musicians aren't particularly interesting. There is not that much that the latest seventeen-year-old who has sold a million records after two weeks locked in the studio with a house full of synthesizers, under the iron discipline of Stock, Aitken, and Waterman, can say or do that is going to keep even the most drooling of fanzines interested for long. Musicians are particularly vulnerable to the swings of fashion because they are so much part of it that they date so quickly. Even Elton John, who at one point in his career was able to command a fee of $3 million from Sasson Industries to sell one of his songs to them for a TV commercial campaign, can no longer take getting into the charts for granted.

The same phenomenon is spreading into other areas. The overnight sensations of the New York art and literature circuit display exactly the same characteristics as the gaudier end of the music business. All too often potential stars such as Sandro Chia and Tama Janowitz are lionized for their first gallery show, or their first book, in the most extravagant of language. They are declared instant geniuses, only to find their second efforts being trashed before they have even had their full fifteen minutes of fame. No sooner have they been declared the latest thing, the essential party guest, the key face to photograph for the magazines, been signed up for deals to endorse lime juice or imported

If it hadn't been Gloria Vanderbilt, it would have been Jackie Kennedy: Warren Hirsch put Vanderbilt's name on Hong Kong jeans and rode the designer jean boom. Now that denim's time has come again, he's renewed his partnership with Vanderbilt

liqueurs, advanced huge sums for their second book or given a restrospective at the Whitney, and made it on to the essential invite list for all the hopeful hot new places in town, than their purpose is served. They are then elbowed aside to make way for the even newer discoveries. Their masterpieces are taken down off the bookshelves and the gallery walls, to go into the attic alongside the hula hoops, the flared trousers, the enamel advertising signs, the victorian pub mirrors, and all those other foolish enthusiasms of mis-spent youth.

As a means of establishing credentials for every conceivable kind of product, the mania for printing, silkscreening, or bolting famous names on to any available surface shows no signs of abating. Some names may become unfashionably obvious through over-use, but others will take their place. And the cult heroes will gracefully grow old, steadily appreciating in prestige and value. As the experiences of the companies that now trade under the names of Chanel and Dior forcefully suggest, when properly looked after great names can easily outlive their original owners, and steadily acquire a deeper encrustation of prestige. So much so that by far the most precious corporate assets of these and many other companies are their names.

Gabrielle Chanel – as Coco was christened – died in 1971. But the revenue from the perfumes that carry her name, and the charisma that goes with them, are as strong as ever. In fact, Chanel had closed her Paris salon in 1939, and had gone into retirement, living on the perfume and jewelry royalties. But such was the residual strength of her name, that she was able to reopen the couture house in 1954 without missing a beat. After her death, the name has been kept alive as a creative force by Karl Lagerfeld, who presides over a policy of resurrecting classic Chanel designs from the company archives, and updating them with subtlety and skill.

In a similar way, the glamour of some of the film stars of the 1950s has turned into an appreciating asset, still being exploited even after their deaths. James Dean's image, for example, is, bizarrely as it turns out, now being licensed by the Curtis Publishing Company of Indianapolis, for use in Krizia's after-shave publicity. The abiding potency of the Dean image, moodily drooping a cigarette from his lower lip, is such that the copy-writers didn't even see fit to identify him in the advertisement, though it is aimed at an audience who would not have been born when Dean made his last film.

Other names can quickly become threadbare. All the pointers seem to suggest that the more precedents there are for an individual trying to come to terms with fame, the more readily it is dealt with, and thereby prolonged. Christian Lacroix, for example, belongs to the third generation of modern fashion stars. In his present incarnation, as the much-touted successor to Dior and Yves St Laurent, he is the careful creation of a finance house that has investigated all the angles to exploiting fame. The lessons of Courrèges and Halston have not gone unnoticed.

First-generation celebrities take things with much less polished ease. The catapulting of a group of obscure billiard-hall snooker aces to international prominence thanks to the sudden discovery of the game by television, caused traumatic personal difficulties for some of the individuals involved. And while several of them may have become wealthy on their winnings and the proceeds of lucrative sponsorship deals, none of them have yet managed to achieve the lasting fame of a cult hero. So far their earning power as celebrities has been limited by the beer-gut and nylon-frilled shirt image of snooker.

There are other overnight celebrities too – not just drawn from the pimply-faced end of the music business – who have been dazzled into a counterproductively greedy approach to the value of their new-found status. You can see it in Michael Graves's fatal inability to say no to even the seediest of offers. He gives the impression that he is terrified that, having become the most celebrated architect of his generation, he is about to be overtaken by younger, fresher talent, and can therefore not afford to say no to any chance of publicity, no matter how tawdry. Ironically, Ralph Lauren, rooted in the rather less intellectually credible fashion business, is much more careful about what he does with his name. He's said no to Lauren cars, Lauren telephones, and Lauren chocolates.

The critical part of maintaining the prestige of a name lies in a well-developed sense of identity, and a clear and well-worked-out strategy about what the name does, and does not, mean. It's vital if the cachet of a hero is not to be diluted by unsuitable associations.

Just as important for the kind of longevity which turns a celebrity into a cult hero is a certain sense of timelessness. The simply fashionable fall quickly by the wayside. The heroes who last are the ones who have the stamina to adapt to adjusting circumstances. Partly it is a question of substance. The cult hero needs to have more than one good idea. But it is also a stylistic issue. What would Jimi Hendrix have looked like in the age of Paul Smith suits and short hair? The iconic images of him are all too rigidly stuck in the late 1960s. The celebrities who have endured are the ones who have been able to modernize themselves, keeping the overall identity intact, but never getting lost in a time warp. Either that, or they have been individuals who have been able to personify more than a single moment in time.

The classic images of Monroe or Dean don't *look* as if they belong to a specific era, in the way that the bizarre extremes of the 1960s – platform soles, cavalier haircuts, elaborate make-up, skin-tight satin flared trousers, and the rest – do. Like all the best cult heroes, they have staying power.

INDEX

Note: Page Numbers in bold type refer to main entries; page numbers in italic type refer to illustrations.